PRAISE FOR *MADE*

"A powerful and practical guide t
of tomorrow's manufacturing cha
business market."

Scott Steinberg, Bestselling Author, *Make Change Work for You*

"This book is a compilation of experiences from manufacturing leaders and experts in Illinois. Some stories may be similar to your own, and others may be new insights about similar issues you are dealing with in your own business. There are plenty of experiences you can learn from and tools you can use to become a more competitive manufacturer in a global market."

Marcia Ayala, President, Aurora Specialty Textiles Group, Inc

---

"At a time of unprecedented change, challenge, and opportunity, the IMEC team has created an extraordinarily solid framework for manufacturers that are hungry to compete and thrive."

Raymond Ziganto, Founder and CEO, Linara International

"Competition is abundant in the business environment. *Made in Illinois* is a powerful tool for managers seeking to cultivate competitive advantage with "off-the-shelf," low-cost strategies for a variety of challenges common to manufacturers. Moreover, *Made in Illinois* balances textbook-like prescriptions with anecdotal experiences from manufacturing executives, providing an added level of relevance to the subject matter. In short, *Made in Illinois* is recommended for any manager who believes her/his company is less than perfect."

Kenneth E. Carlton, Vice President, Corrugated Metals, Inc.

"Early in *Made in Illinois*, the Illinois Manufacturing Excellence Center makes the point: "Our generation now faces another crossroad moment." While directed at manufacturers, *Made in Illinois* should be read by a much broader audience. The insights and practical advice offered through a series of chapters will help not only those in manufacturing, but also policymakers and others who care about our economic future and determining how best to navigate this crossroad moment."

Dan Berglund, President and CEO, SSTI

"Illinois is an epicenter of manufacturing intelligence and experience. The breadth and depth of the various manufacturing sectors is fertile ground for building out books such as this and with so much utility for the reader. The team at IMEC have done a spectacular job of codifying the challenges that Illinois manufacturers have faced, and at the same time, they have identified the solutions that can be brought to bare for manufacturers the world around. Readers will be delighted by the pace and depth of what should be required reading for manufacturers and professionals that are driven to elevate their business and accelerate their success."

Jeff Taylor, President and CEO, Crafts Technology

"The success story of US Manufacturing was built on adaptability and resilience. IMEC has proven itself to be stewards of both, and they will continue to be an education and networking hub for Illinois manufacturers for decades to come. There's no better way to stay current on tech, trends, and best practices in the industry."

Aneesa Muthana, CEO and Co-Owner, Pioneer Service Inc.

"*Made in Illinois* is a positive take on manufacturing informed by the lessons learned from folks who work with thousands of manufacturers annually throughout Illinois. It is easily accessible and worth a few hours to read. I hope it sparks reflection and rethinking how leaders lead. The book places leadership at the fulcrum for manufacturers as they confront the short-term challenges brought on by the COVID-19 pandemic and the long-term challenges facing manufacturing in light of workforce issues, global competition, advances in technology as they pivot to maintain their competitive edge. It provides important insights into the importance of leadership in addressing the multi-faceted challenges facing all manufacturers and sage advice and counsel for current and future manufacturing leaders. It is a must-read for manufacturing leaders in Illinois and beyond."

Kenneth P. Voytek, Principal, Mountain View Economics and formerly Chief Economist at NIST MEP

"*Made in Illinois* is an engaging, succinct, and timely playbook for manufacturers in Illinois. Suitable for use as a team resource or a development guide, the concise volume is worth the investment of your time."

Steve Rauschenberger, President, Technology and Manufacturing Association

---

"A helpful guide on how to improve operations, cultivate a high-performing team, and win in the global manufacturing landscape. Dave has captured his team's most important and relevant advice for manufacturing leaders into one easy-to-read playbook."

Michelle Drew Rodriguez, VP of Strategy and Corporate Development, Tenneco

---

"As an author and forty-year veteran of our industry, I am impressed by the people interviewed–several of whom are long-standing, highly respected customers of mine. Their insight and experiences transform this playbook into an enduring masterpiece we can all learn from. What has been missing in our industry is a "HOW-TO PLAYBOOK" that allows everyone to understand how to engage in a proactive path to resolve the many workforce challenges we face in our factories, out on the shop floor, in our offices, and throughout. It is encouraging to see IMEC join the fight in "Finding America's Greatest Champion." I applaud Made in Illinois. Just as Iverson & Company has endured for more than 90 years, I am confident this book will take us into the next, new frontier of manufacturing."

Terry M. Iverson, President of Iverson & Company, author of *Finding America's Greatest Champion,* and founder of ChampionNow!

"*Made In Illinois* is a wonderful tool for manufacturers as they look to help their organizations and employees thrive in a post-COVID world and economy. Each section promotes thoughtful self-review and provides actionable steps that can be implemented by companies of any size. If you are a manufacturing manager, this book should be shared across your organization."

Tom Welge, Vice President of Technical Sales, Gilster-Mary Lee Corporation

"Whether it was the Civil War, the Industrial Revolution, advent of the assembly line, or the global response to the coronavirus pandemic, Illinois manufacturing has played a key role in nearly every major historical event in our nation's history. Today, manufacturers have created an innovation engine that is reshaping the world around us and leading the charge into the 21st century digital economy with pioneering breakthroughs in machine learning, 5G, robotics, artificial intelligence, augmented reality, and the Internet of Things. *Made in Illinois* is a wonderful new compilation of writings from the Illinois Manufacturing Excellence Center and leading manufacturers eager to share their lessons, experiences, and leadership to help the next generation of manufacturers succeed. Leaders across all sectors can find valuable stories that will foster excellence for our state's creators and makers, dreamers and doers."

Mark Denzler, President and CEO, Illinois Manufacturers' Association

---

"IMEC is a powerful organization that has helped so many companies in the state of Illinois become globally competitive manufacturers. The IMEC team has a wealth of expertise and they have put that knowledge down on paper to give a playbook for leaders to use. Thank you IMEC for writing this book!"

Craig Van den Avont, President, GAM Enterprises, Inc.

"My experience with IMEC goes back for at least a decade. I learned of them through my manufacturing association, TMA, of which CARR has been a member of since 1973, and I served as their chairman in 2016-2017. IMEC has been on the leading edge of assisting small and medium-sized manufacturing companies with resources that are aligned with and benefit us all and who otherwise wouldn't realize this assistance was available to them. Most recently, we engaged with the IMEC team to do a comprehensive shop floor layout of our new facility in order to have a structured and proactive roadmap on placement of existing machinery and the future of the shop floor. It was both a pleasure and good fortune to have worked with these professionals, and I am confident it will not be the last time."

Jim Carr, President, CARR Machine & Tool, Inc.

"I relate especially to two priorities from this book: workforce and supply chains. Both declined in the US from 2000 until 2010. Both are now coming back. The two are tightly related. We need a higher quantity and quality of workforce to compete and produce the work being reshored. Higher productivity then enables more reshoring, repairing supply chain gaps, and attracting more high potential recruits."

Harry C. Moser, Founder and President, Reshoring Initiative®

"There were some great HEROES identified during the pandemic and manufacturers were high on the list! Our manufacturers went OVER THE TOP to get everything MADE IN ILLINOIS this year, but guess what? They do that EVERY year! As things evolve and our companies figure out the new game, politically, economically, and culturally, it's nice to know IMEC is there with resources like your new *Made in Illinois, A Modern Playbook for Manufacturers.* One of my favorite parts of this excellent playbook was the simplicity of what should be the most important focus–People, Performance and Mindset–with tactical advice. Thank you, Dr. Boulay and team, for always supporting our special people. We appreciate your dedication."

Kathy Gilmore, President, Valley Industrial Association

MADE IN ILLINOIS

A MODERN PLAYBOOK FOR MANUFACTURERS TO COMPETE AND WIN

MADE IN ILLINOIS

Cover design by Kristy Johns
Layout by Manuel Serna

For more information, contact:
Fig Factor Media | www.figfactormedia.com
IMEC | www.imec.org

Printed in the United States of America

ISBN: 978-1-952779-07-7

Library of Congress Control Number: 2021900959

TABLE OF CONTENTS

PREFACE: PLAYING THE LONG GAME

by David Boulay, President of IMEC

. . . IT IS THE INTEREST OF A COMMUNITY, WITH A VIEW TO EVENTUAL AND PERMANENT ECONOMY, TO ENCOURAGE THE GROWTH OF MANUFACTURES.

-*Alexander Hamilton,* Report on Manufactures,1791[1]

Manufacturing ignites our senses. The sights, touches, sounds, and smells of making things captivate us. Today's production technologies are alive with seemingly limitless motions to spin, shave, assemble, fill, measure, move, label, and package all the manufactured items in our lives. We are mesmerized by the technologies, framed with painted floors and bright lighting, that are sequenced to create the transformative nature of manufacturing. Making things is a uniquely human venture that sits deep in our psyche. The sensory experiences of manufacturing light up our brains.

Manufacturers are innovators and creators who have long spurred societal progress. The Industrial Revolution (1760-1820) was the transition to new manufacturing processes in the United States and Europe. Alexander Hamilton understood the significance of manufacturing as the economic growth engine needed in the new country, and some of his policies and ideas spurred that growth. The late 1700s was indeed a pivotal moment for makers. Yet, archaeologists keep uncovering the many ways our maker spirit has been producing for over a million years. Our earliest ancestors manufactured boats, spears, hooks, chisels, hammers, pottery, and toys, as well as ritual and decorative embellishments. We learned to control fire into heat processes and to invent the wheel as the means to produce with the potter's wheel. Being makers is in our DNA.

The makers of the past would be overwhelmed by the ways we produce today. The manufactured goods that roll off our production floors are marvels created by people and technology working together. Every car passing on the road is a collection of 30,000 perfectly-fitted parts performing a high-intensity coordinated task with ease. The cell phone's simplicity belies its complexity of eyeglass quality screens, mini-circuitry, antenna capability, microphones, speakers, batteries, and the case to hold it all together in our hand. The products we create are shaping society in unimaginable ways.

Illinois is a manufacturing powerhouse. Illinois has a rich manufacturing tradition and offers vast assets and strengths. Given the blend of technology and innovation hubs (like Argonne National Laboratory and Fermilab), a world-class transportation infrastructure, over 192 higher education institutions, and a well-educated workforce, there is little surprise that over 12,400 manufacturers and 37 Fortune 500 firms call Illinois home. Illinois manufacturing is well-diversified with over 572,000 people creating products used in every facet of society: chemical, food, machinery, fabricated metal, plastics, electronic products, pharmaceutical, and so much more. Illinois is well integrated in the global economy, representing the 17th largest economy in the world at the time of publishing this book.

The Essence of Manufacturing

Today's manufacturing companies produce their modern-day marvels through a mind-boggling and wide-ranging set of knowledge and abilities. Critical to success are the ways leaders bring their entrepreneurial spirit to assemble and nurture a team of unique and complementary talents. This team applies its abilities to use technologies and continuously increase performance to stay ahead of customer requests and the competition. In some form, every company addresses strategy, leadership, customers, operations, workforce, and knowledge management as processes that lock together like gears to drive success. Groups of individuals apply their talents toward a common focus, creating the production outputs that meet the societal needs of their time.

Victory comes from a leader's mindset and overall direction or strategy to create sustained positive customer relationships. Accomplishment comes from selecting and nurturing the right suppliers and hiring, training, and engaging a team. Triumph occurs through the operational know-how to design products and solutions, apply technologies, and manage processes for peak performance. The leader's mindset pulls it all together, reflects on past performance, deals with today's results, and prepares for the future.

People, performance, and mindset have remained enduring foundations of manufacturing.

Facing a Crossroad: A Moment for Makers to Lead

Every generation stands at a crossroad due to massive societal challenges. Economic shocks, pandemics, war, famine, and natural disasters, among others, reshape society. These are critical decision moments for business leaders. We can decide to wait for things to get back to normal or we can decide to respond and embrace change. Our generation now faces another crossroad moment.

The Great Recession and the pandemic were the one-two punch over the last decade. These events have caused us to rethink every element of how we make things in our country. The Great Recession quietly laid bare an underlying competitive crisis for US manufacturing. Productivity flattened and declined even though we experienced a decade-long economic rebound from unquestionably the worst downturn since the Great Depression. This productivity stall adversely affected our ability to compete globally and improve our standard of living.

The pandemic hit with a force not seen in over a century. In a few short weeks, it reshaped most facets of everyday life and business. Manufacturing leaders needed to determine their responses for workplace health and safety, employment, legal implications, supply chain resilience, demand fluctuation, revenue pressures, related cash flow pains, and workplace redesign such as remote work and social distancing on a production line. Perhaps the greatest challenge has been the enduring uncertainty and lack of visibility.

Crossroad moments spur innovation, collective thinking, collaboration, and grit. We evaluate and reset our patterns of thinking. We improve how best to fulfill our business mission and create new ways of making things. It's what makers have always done. This crossroad moment gave the IMEC team the opportunity to create and assemble solutions and guidance to manufacturers during a pivotal time. Thus, the book you see before you, a collection of insights pulled together in one place as a playbook designed for you.

How to Use This Book

Made in Illinois, compiled from IMEC's collective writings over time, is meant to inspire you to rethink excellence within your company. For you, each week is hectic. Working in the business while also trying to improve the business is not easy. While it may feel like you're running a race by yourself sometimes, *Made in Illinois* is your pit crew and guide. You will hear peer and expert voices who fully understand your experience. Their insights will energize your efforts to remain on the global stage as an enduring competitor.

One approach we took to writing the book was to explore the essential elements of manufacturing success. Every company aims to leverage leadership and strategy to better focus on customers and align operational performance, workforce talent, and knowledge management. As efforts such as the US Department of Commerce NIST Baldrige performance excellence program has long demonstrated, these are powerful aspects of business success. We frame these elements into three parts: people, performance, and mindset. Within these categories, we share best practices, insights, lessons learned, and questions to inspire new thoughts.

Makers are doers. We want action. This book is a call to action, bringing new ideas into your business. I encourage you to read *Made in Illinois* with your team. Pass it along to others. It's fitting for a regular book club with each short section serving as a topical discussion over coffee. Discuss what you learn. Use it as a guide to find the relevant nuggets for your company. Take notes. Identify your strengths, and celebrate even the smallest achievements. List out as many opportunities for improvement ideas as you can. At the end, narrow the list into five actions you will take. Identify gaps, rethink the way you do things, and act upon change. I guarantee others will.

Manufacturing resides at the forefront of progress and lays the foundation for future direction. Together, we will face forward to the future and create stronger, more successful companies. As you explore topics related to people, performance, and mindset, may it inspire manufacturing excellence for your company and ensure productivity and innovation that leads you to greater global competitiveness.

PART 1: PEOPLE

We start where all great things start in life: with people. People drive our competitive positioning—from our teams in every corner of our company to supply chain partners to customers. Our community of people extends far beyond those closest to us and includes board members, influencers, mentors, investors, media, association partners, education, and our networks. In Part 1, we will explore opportunities to strengthen human connections and thereby strengthen our competitive stature as Illinois manufacturers. We begin with you, a leader with vision, passion, and good intentions on making your company—whether small, large, or in between—a true innovator in the twenty-first century. Onward and upward, together . . .

Chapter 1

LEADERS, HOW DO YOU DEFINE EXCELLENCE?

Play to your greatest strengths.

A day in the life of an Illinois manufacturer is like a giant machine with many working gears all turning at once. You must produce product, take care of customers, manage processes, keep the website updated, manage supplier relationships, write proposals and estimates, complete compliance audits, train employees, and so much more.

Amidst these demands, you also have to think about growth. While day-to-day tasks are fairly easy to define, growth requires us to envision where we want our organizations to be at some point in the future. At IMEC, we consider the progress in between as a journey toward excellence and, ultimately, organizational success. The path requires exploring, learning, and optimizing a manufacturing company's key success drivers: leadership, strategy, customers, workforce, operations, and measurements of results.

High performing manufacturers naturally strive for organizational success. Like a professional athlete, you take action to strengthen your organization, positioning it as a fierce competitor. In pursuit of organizational success, your organization becomes more resilient. You are ready for just about anything because, as we all know, even the best five-year plans can be bested within minutes when unexpected shifts in the market or sudden disruption takes root.

Speaking of disruption, a few things have changed for the world at large because of the pandemic, and we would be remiss if we did not point this out. At the time of publishing this book, vaccines are being distributed, but even if the pandemic were to officially end tomorrow (wouldn't that be something to pop the champagne over), manufacturing leaders will continue to deal with the aftereffects a prolonged pandemic has brought to operations, staff, and supply chains. Our hope is that *Made in Illinois* will help you manage through and exit this pandemic stronger than before and safeguard your company for years to come with strong crisis management skills and gritty readiness.

When we talk about organizational success, we begin with a general overview or "snapshot" of your company, otherwise known as your organizational profile. If you're doing the eye roll, we get it. How many SWOT analyses must you do, you ask ever so politely? Rest assured, we do not mean creating intense deliverables like a technology audit or a step-by-step instructional manual of every process you have in place. Rather, understanding your path to organizational success means looking inward and taking stock of your organization from two perspectives:

- What are your key organizational characteristics?
- What is your organization's strategic situation? (Ask: what are your goals, who is aware of your current goals, what departments are included, and how often is your organizational strategy updated?)
- In the spirit of being a playbook, you could also ask: what "game" are you playing, how will you win, and who are you really playing against?

On the surface, these questions seem simple enough. Here's the thing: ask five or more people in your company these same questions and then jot down their answers. Do they match? Are they consistent? If they aren't, that's OK. It just means defining organizational success more succinctly is important for everyone to move in the same direction.

Organizational success impacts global competitiveness. According to a report by McKinsey Global Institute, emerging markets are an unfolding trend for manufacturers:

> *By 2025, overall global consumption is forecast to reach $62 trillion, twice its 2013 level, and fully half of this increase will come from the emerging world. In 2010, the "consuming class"—people with disposable incomes of more than $10 a day—had 2.4 billion members, just over a third of the world's population. By 2025, that will rise to more than half. Taking population growth into account, there will be an extra 1.8 billion consumers, the vast majority living in emerging regions.*[2]

> *For manufacturers, the story is even more compelling. We estimate that emerging markets will be the destination for 65 percent of the world's manufactured goods by 2025. Consumption starts with the basics, and the purchase of capital-intensive goods (such as cars, building products, and machinery) is driving the shift.*[3]

McKinsey Global Institute is not alone in its projections. In fact, by 2050, "economies like Indonesia, Brazil, and Mexico are likely to be bigger than those of the United Kingdom and France." The seven largest emerging markets can grow approximately two times as fast as advanced economies, such as the United States. Six of the seven largest economies in the world are projected to be emerging economies by 2050.[4]

Like exports, cost competitiveness also positions companies for a global foothold. According to the BCG Global Manufacturing Cost Competitiveness Index, the US has made significant strides "against 18 of the world's 38 biggest manufacturing export economies in 2018—reversing a recent trend—even though the once-large US cost advantage in energy has waned. The reason: manufacturing productivity leaped by 4% in 2018, compared with a 2% increase the previous year."[5]

One other interesting outtake from the study was the direct correlation between investing in productivity and competitiveness. According to the report, "European economies that have underinvested in productivity—such as France, Italy, and Spain—became less cost competitive in 2018, while manufacturing productivity gains in Germany and Finland enabled those economies to maintain their competitiveness."

Road mapping organizational success can be challenging. A manufacturer in operation for a half century with fifty or so employees runs on getting things done. There may be little time for working "on" the business. For the manufacturer with multiple facilities and a growing team, going back and reassessing your company needs is an easy step to miss, even though much has most likely changed drastically since the early days of the organization. Understanding where you are today while forging a path toward a clear vision becomes a straight line to achieving goals. Organizational success drives great companies forward, providing a definitive map that puts your team, customers, and suppliers on the same page.

In this chapter, you will explore that definitive map in detail with questions to help you gain a better understanding of your organizational success. You will also learn about effective communication practices when time is of the essence, the powerful role of trust, and how the manufacturing CEO can build a culture of confidence through diversity and inclusion. Lastly, you'll have a front row seat to a conversation with Robert Barnett, former executive vice president for Motorola.

PURSUING ORGANIZATIONAL SUCCESS

Illinois manufacturers competing to win globally will be among those that carefully consider organizational success, performance, and results by shifting from a tactical to a more strategic approach. What's the first step? Where do you begin? Connecting future decisions to meet a goal starts with knowing what you have to work with.

Let's unpack this.

Many organizations are structured around operations, finance, and sales. Sales creates demand, operations process said demand for products and services, and finance takes care of the money.

External pressures, like quality and cost reductions, drive the need for improved efficiency in organizations. To address this pressure, many have applied continuous improvement efforts. Continuous improvement seeks to improve every process in your company by enhancing value-added activities for your customer while removing as many waste activities as possible. For many, there is a focus around operations to include 5S workplace organization (a system to organize your workplace based on sort, set in order, shine, standardize, and sustain–more on this later), process flow, facility layouts, quality, inventory control, and workforce and skills development.

Here's the big takeaway: taking stock of your organizational characteristics and strategy fuels competitive advantage. This concept has its roots in Japan with the country's prestigious Deming Prize, which was launched in 1951 as a way to recognize Japanese-style Total Quality

Management (TQM).[6] The story: Dr. W. E. Deming was an American quality control expert who visited Japan to lead an "Eight-Day Course on Quality Control" at the Auditorium of the Japan Medical Association in Kanda-Surugadai, Tokyo, as well as a follow-up seminar in Hakone. His presentation materials were then packaged and sold for a fee. The managing director of the Union of Japanese Scientists and Engineers (JUSE) was so grateful, he proposed naming the award after Dr. Deming as a symbol of his contribution and generous spirit.

Some three decades after the Deming Prize, the US debuted their own Total Quality Recognition Award, the Malcolm Baldrige National Quality Award, giving manufacturers in the US the "Baldrige challenge" for excellence. According to the award's website, it turned out that the award itself is secondary because, as it points out, the "true payoff comes from the journey."[7]

This approach is more comprehensive than the traditional focus on operations, finance, and sales, or even continuous improvement. Instead, it focuses on a path to organizational success.

The book you are holding in your hands is not about the Baldrige Award. Nor is it meant to provide a treatise on quality. Rather, it is a playbook of ideas and best practices on how you, the Illinois manufacturer, can better compete and win on a global scale.

By exploring your company's strengths and opportunities for improvement in these six categories, you'll step out of the day-to-day and harness the power of strategic thinking:

1. **Leadership.** How do senior leaders' personal actions and responsibilities and your governance system guide and sustain the organization to build success now and into the future?
2. **Strategy.** How do you develop strategic objectives and action plans, implement them, change them if required, and measure progress?
3. **Customers.** How do you engage customers for long-term success, listen to customers, serve your customers, and exceed expectations and build customer relationships?
4. **Workforce.** What workforce practices are utilized to create and maintain a high-performance environment? How will you engage your workforce and your organization to adapt to change? How will your workforce succeed as a team?
5. **Operations.** How do you focus on your organization's work, product design and delivery, innovation, and operational effectiveness to achieve success now and in the future?
6. **Measurement and Results.** How do you measure, analyze, and improve organizational performance to align your operation with strategic objectives?

From this, consider the above areas from four distinct perspectives:

- **Approach.** What is your approach in each of these areas? Who will contribute to the approach?

- **Deployment.** How is that approach being deployed? Is it aligned, effective, and systematic? How do you know?
- **Learning.** What new knowledge or skills have been acquired or learned that has improved the approach? How do you know you've gotten better? Is it a fact-based systematic manner with evidence of organizational learning?
- **Integration.** Has the organization achieved a state of consistency and harmonization of all the individual components of a performance management system that operates as a fully interconnected unit?

Baldrige demands a holistic view of the organization, requiring alignment across all areas. It engages the entire leadership team to collaborate and cooperate through a strategically focused approach. This positions an organization to succeed and compete more fiercely.

"The journey" as was pointed out earlier, then takes on a transformational magic. The knowledge gained trickles down to impact employees at all levels and drives a new, forward-thinking culture with stronger employee engagement. Organizational success goes beyond sales, operations, and financial models. The larger focus is on continuous improvement that catapults an organization to a level of consistent performance. A thoughtful plan going forward will empower your people, performance, and mindset as a global competitor. In the following sections, we'll look at best practices to achieve organizational success.

THE ROAD TO BUILDING TRUST

It's hard to be a leader. You have people relying on you who are sometimes worried about their jobs, their families, or their financial situation.

Building trust within your organization relieves some of your employees' stress–and maybe even some of your own.

To establish trust, inspire a culture of open communication by being vulnerable and honest. Your actions must match your words. If you commit to something, do it. If you ask an employee to follow a certain protocol, then you, too, must be willing to follow that same protocol. Establishing trust also requires use of the Key Principles, as presented in Development Dimensions International leadership training modules.[8] They are as follows:

- Maintaining or enhancing self-esteem
- Listening and responding with empathy
- Asking for help and encouraging involvement
- Sharing thoughts, feelings, and rationale to build trust
- Providing support without removing responsibility to build a sense of ownership

Perhaps the most important point from above is empathy. Acknowledge the hardships many employees face on a daily basis. You can share your feelings and concerns (just be careful not to overshare) because by sharing a bit about how you are coping (or not), you are demonstrating that you are human, giving employees permission to relax and realize they are not alone in whatever they are experiencing.

Overcommunicating is rarely negative. An absence of information makes people worry. If we don't regularly hear from the person we report to, even if nothing has changed, it is easy to worry that there is something wrong. In a vacuum we tend to allow our minds to make things up. Usually, we go to the "dark side" and make up all kinds of worst-case scenarios. This is how the rumor mill gets started and keeps going. We say to ourselves, "If they aren't telling me anything, everything must be very bad."

Consider sending short emails to everyone on a regular basis, posting to an internal employee website, or recording a brief message that you can upload to YouTube. A video message can be particularly impactful since your employees can see you and connect with your image as well as your message.

Build trust. Communicate openly and honestly. Your employees will respect you and work to support you and the business as best they can.

This level of trust and transparency builds the future and becomes a new business currency by which to chart a course toward organizational success. Senior leadership communication, sharing timely information throughout the company, transparency in governance, and informing your community chart the path to creating a culture where communication is a priority.

COMMUNICATION AND THE ART OF LISTENING

As we saw in the previous section, communication is an important trust builder. In fact, when we ask supervisors about some of the problems they face, "communication" is nearly always raised as a key issue. This seemingly simple response can lead to a complex question: how do we improve communication?

Here are four methods for communicating that contribute to a stronger organizational DNA.

Provide an ongoing feedback loop. At the time of this writing, some workers may be doing assignments remotely. Regardless of where your workforce is, keep productivity levels high by continuing to practice timely, balanced, and specific feedback.[9] Consider the following points to create a feedback loop:'

- Timely positive feedback strongly reinforces positive actions and results.
- Timely developmental feedback provides suggestions soon enough for people to adjust and enhance their performance.
- Create balanced feedback that focuses on both what the person can improve upon as well as how the person is being successful.
- Be specific when providing feedback by informing the person what they accomplished and how it positively impacted the organization.

Have meaningful and consistent check-ins with employees. Workers who feel they are being heard by others are 4.6 times more likely to feel empowered to perform their best, which ultimately increases quality productivity levels.[10] Consider the following points to have more meaningful conversations:

- Perform check-ins to allow for people to feel heard. When you have a workforce that is heard, the workers feel motivated. They feel they can make an impact.
- When checking in, show empathy for others (96% of workers have indicated when empathy is shown, employee retention is advanced).[11]
- Invite various people to the table to ensure diversity and inclusion.

Be honest and transparent. Transparency is the new business currency, and it starts at the top. When leaders follow through on promises, provide honest feedback, and emphasize ethical behavior, a culture of trust takes root. We just mentioned trust, but it is important enough to repeat. Consider this: a total of 35% of workers would leave their company if they didn't trust their managers.[12] When leaders tell the whole truth, they allow for relevant information to be shared and relationships to grow stronger. The following are steps to have a clear and transparent conversation:

- Be open-minded.
- Create a clear purpose around a given discussion so everyone understands its importance.

- Continuously seek and share information about a situation or task that is occurring, explore the scope, and clarify expectations.
- Involve others by asking for additional ideas.
- Develop an action plan to address the situation at hand.
- Close the conversation by providing a high-level overview of the plan. Do this while being a confident and positive leader.

Practice the art of listening. We are taught to read and write, yet listening is our most used communications tool (45% compared to 16% for reading and 9% for writing). Listening with the intent to hear and not listening with the intent to respond is learned art. Improving listening skills will sharpen communication skills. Consider these ideas to amp up your listening skills.

- **Define the problem further.** Apply root cause analysis to the actual problem being discussed. Is this communication for the purpose of providing information or for solving a problem, or asking a question or for helping someone improve? What is the importance of the problem?
- **Effective communication is a two-way street.** In order for a message to be conveyed, first it has to be sent, then it has to be accepted. Hearing is just one piece of the sensory experience of listening. You can hear someone talk without tuning into their specific message. This typically happens when a person is looking at their phone while someone is talking.

- **Listening requires every bit of us being engaged in the act of taking in the message.** We need to hear with our ears, but we also need to see with our eyes. And if we can't see with our eyes, we need to be particularly in tune with any vocal tones and changes. As we shed assumptions and embrace the needs of others, we also keep in mind that those with nontraditional communication needs due to a disability may need other cues or accommodations to listen well.
- **Listening well means being open to understanding the other person.** Think of a time when you have communicated with someone you just met versus talking to someone you have known for a long time. It's difficult to interpret pauses and inflections and phrases with a new person, so we may have to listen more carefully as we get to know that person's unique sense of humor, expressions, and style.
- **Listening for tone extends to the written word.** Tone is how something is said. Think of the last time you received an email that wasn't quite clear and maybe created hard feelings due to a misunderstanding. Tone can become easily misunderstood. We can't see the expressions on the other person's face when we are emailing or texting with them. We can only "hear their tone" through words. When a quick and reliable response is needed, especially in times when emotions may run higher than normal, understanding our tone and interpreting the tone of others becomes an imperative in the art of listening. Ask for clarification after a conversation.

How well an organization communicates impacts how we regard an employer or brand. Think about the different types of environments you have worked in. Most likely, you can describe an organization, with tremendous accuracy, on how well people communicated. We might describe, for example, our workplace with a phrase like "nobody ever listens when I give new ideas" or, on a much brighter note, "I can always speak my mind." Effective communication is an imperative when a quick response is needed, which is oftentimes the case in manufacturing, where demands can change on the daily.

WHAT ABRAHAM LINCOLN TEACHES US ABOUT INSPIRING A CULTURE OF CONFIDENCE AND LOYALTY

This wouldn't be a book about leadership in Illinois without mentioning Abraham Lincoln! Published in 1992 and written by Donald T. Phillips, the little paperback *Lincoln on Leadership* is a profound, timeless reminder of the simple, yet effective things we can do every day to build an organizational culture where confidence and loyalty thrive. Here is where you explore the much sought-after quality of endurance, a true point of strength to competing globally.

Through the lessons Illinois native Lincoln shows us, let's reframe our thinking and reset our motivation to lead with a broader perspective. (And, if Lincoln is too far back for you, Google the Deepwater Horizon Oil Spill of 2010, Memorable Gulf Coast Hurricanes, or Johnson and Johnson and Tylenol in 1982. These examples of great leadership in times of crisis will inspire you to persevere as well).

First, consider this point by Phillips: "Only ten days before Abraham Lincoln took office, the Confederate States of America seceded from the Union, taking Federal agencies, forts and arsenals with them." In the heat of conflict and national strife, Lincoln became one of our most honored and revered presidents in history.

Lincoln's stalwart leadership provides valuable lessons for today on how you, too, can build confidence and loyalty among your workforce and unite under a more focused mission.

Four key lessons provide the backdrop for working with people, acting with character, taking decisive action, and that ever popular topic we've already explored, but cannot overcommunicate, communication.

As a leader, be accessible to your people. Lincoln was accessible to his people. He believed that accessibility of the leader would build trust. When people know they *genuinely* have easy access to their leader, they'll tend to view their leader as more trustworthy.

Amid the rapidly shifting sea changes unfolding around you, how are you, as a leader, genuinely creating easy access to sustain and maintain trust? How are you gathering and listening to ideas and suggestions? Instead of sequestering himself as the top dog who knew all the answers, Lincoln formed successful alliances with others to bring the maximum amount of wisdom to bear in every situation. He was a good listener.

What methods are you using to maintain accessibility?

At IMEC, our president, David Boulay, hosts weekly team huddles as well as frequent open discussion forums, all through IMEC's virtual networks. Although many of us are working from home, we have ample opportunities to feel connected.

As a leader, act with character. Most of us are familiar with the phrase "Honest Abe." This lesson focuses on the importance of being honest, acting with integrity, articulating the values of the organization in visible, behavior-based terms, and showing compassion for others. From his earliest days as a shopkeeper in New Salem, Illinois, Lincoln developed a reputation for honesty and fairness. Employees who feel their leader is misleading them or withholding information from them begin to gossip and complain. In the absence of trusted information, rumors circulate quickly, especially in challenging times.

As a leader, check in with yourself every day to determine whether or not you are holding yourself to high standards. You are the key to pulling the organization toward hopeful outcomes, not spreading misinformation and fear. If you are attacked, and this is common simply by virtue of your position, do what Honest Abe did: ignore attacks on your character, but hold fast to your sense of humor and "doing the right thing."

Consider this: many companies today are being asked to change their production processes and even the products they produce for the good of the whole. A strong leader of character demonstrates commitment to the good of the whole by helping the organization pivot to a higher and more immediate calling. People will follow you through tumultuous change when your reputation precedes you.

Phillips sums it up when he says, "Any leader can learn from Abraham Lincoln's standards. He had great confidence in his own competence and ability to perform. He was not insecure and did not feel threatened by others. He was also flexible, open-minded, and willing to let his subordinates take the glory for their victories."

As a leader, take decisive action. Even at a time in history when countless lives and the fate of the nation was at stake, Lincoln had the will and the ability to make tough decisions when necessary. He did not procrastinate or hesitate and, therefore, his decisiveness enacted extraordinary change. Solid decision-making is a requirement of leadership, because the most well-crafted vision will be worthless without decisive action to accomplish it. When leaders waffle and postpone, valuable time is lost, and competitors gain the edge. Be fair but do it in a timely manner. The book continues: "Sit back? Wait to see if someone else comes forward to handle the problem? Not so for Lincoln."

This lesson also points out that Lincoln was a catalyst for change. He learned early in his presidency that he'd have to rebuild and reorganize the government and its armed forces. We need leaders who are continually seeking innovative ideas that lead to solutions. Lincoln was continually looking for ways to remake the system rather than resign himself to the problems and the flaws he knew about. Instead, he worked with his colleagues and others to find new solutions and create a climate of "risk-free entrepreneurship necessary to foster effective innovation." What a much-needed quality today!

What actions are you currently taking to foster an environment of innovation and problem-solving in your organization? Who is following your lead?

As a leader, communicate. What book on leadership would be complete without talking about communication? We speak with many frontline supervisors who rate communication as a top priority. Phillips speaks to Lincoln's abilities as a humble, but exceptionally effective public speaker and his ability to use words to create meaning and vision for his followers. Lincoln frequently used stories and anecdotes, colloquial expressions, symbols, and imagery to persuade. Lincoln also moved others with more than just his words. He walked his talk. His actions mirrored what he said. In other words, do what you say and say what you do.

Instead of making a demand, Lincoln would relate a well-chosen story to persuade others. Sometimes he would tell stories or write letters to support and encourage the people around him. This week, write a hand-written note to a colleague to thank them for their hard work. We all treasure these messages and hang onto them for many years. When it is all said and done, any business setbacks or disruptions will provide many stories of resilience, agility, and acts of courage. As leaders, these can be opportunities to inspire others to become more confident and committed to organizational success.

HOW THE MODERN MANUFACTURING CEO IS DRIVING DIVERSITY AND INCLUSION

To close out this chapter exploring leadership and organizational excellence, we take a deeper dive into diversity and inclusion (D&I). The precedent you set as a leader defines D&I for the entire organization.

In concert with the Manufacturing Institute, PwC published a report entitled "Five Paths to Making Diversity and Inclusion Work."[13] The report includes many perspectives with a resounding conclusion that D&I is a "core business goal."

Michelle Murphy, Chief Diversity Officer and VP, Global Talent, at Ingersoll Rand, points to the role of the company's CEO in the report:

> "Diversity and inclusion is led by our CEO. He sets the tone at the top with his leadership and expects every leader in the company to help advance our diversity and inclusion goals and lead by example. We don't treat D&I as an HR issue, rather it is embraced as a business strategy; how our company grows is just as important as the growth we achieve."

Many agree, however, that manufacturing as an industry is playing catch-up when it comes to D&I initiatives.

Let's first take a look at these terms. The Merriam-Webster dictionary defines diversity as "the inclusion of different types of people in a group or organization." While race and gender are obvious demographic points of difference, a diverse workplace could include people of different religions, sexual orientation, age, hometowns, education, or physical abilities.

In contrast, inclusion refers to a cultural feeling of belonging. Again, we turn to Merriam-Webster for this definition: "the act or practice of including and accommodating people who have historically been excluded (as because of their race, gender, sexuality, or ability)."

While the two terms stand side-by-side, a diverse organization does not automatically mean inclusion exists.

The outcomes from D&I are extraordinary. Many statistics show a direct relationship between D&I and higher profitability, increased innovation, and a better talent pipeline. When employees feel valued, they are more engaged, which leads to greater productivity and a willingness to work harder so the whole team wins. Check out these stats:

- Inclusive teams improve team performance by up to 30% in high-diversity environments.[14]
- Higher representation of women in C-suite positions results in 34% greater returns to shareholders.[15]
- So, what does D&I mean to Illinois manufacturers? Opportunity.

You now have the opportunity to change the long-standing perception that manufacturing is not a viable option for women and minorities. This directly impacts recruitment of talent, access to new markets and customers, sharing of diverse opinions and ideas, and awareness around unconscious bias. Based on data provided by the Bureau of Labor Statistics, we know that, of the approximately 13,000 manufacturers in Illinois, there are only 64 Black-owned businesses. We also know that while 50% of the workforce is composed of women, only 29.4% of the manufacturing workforce nationwide is comprised of women.[16]

More on this topic later. In chapter two, you will see an illuminating conversation about D&I with Katherine Ramsey and Kris Cuthbertson from G&W Electric.

For now, let's figure out where to start. Most manufacturers that are small and midsize are unable to have a dedicated D&I director. Here are five simple steps to consider in your business strategy:

- Make D&I a priority at the C-suite level.
- Explore unconscious bias in your job ads and hiring practices.
- Educate people across the company about unconscious bias and the impact it has on people, culture, and productivity.
- Consider scorecards that measure D&I practices.
- Survey people about how they feel empowered, valued, and heard.
- Share D&I topics in your company newsletter.
- Add a board member with D&I expertise or make D&I a discussion topic at the board level.
- Create a D&I statement.

THE BIG PLAY: STRATEGY

A Conversation with Robert Barnett, former Executive Vice President for Motorola and IMEC Board Member

Before retirement, Robert "Bob" Barnett spent thirteen years as an executive at Motorola and he has not stopped contributing to the Illinois economy since. Barnett spends his time on many boards and organizations, including IMEC's board, where he has helped fine-tune our own organizational success.

Barnett sat down with us virtually to discuss strategy. "Strategy is where we are now, where we want to be in a year, where we want to be in three to five years," Barnett explained when looking back at both his work on Motorola's leadership team and his work since then, helping other organizations thrive.

"There are two pieces [to strategy] that I look at when I see corporations doing well. The first is, how do you develop the strategy? That is, what do you write down on a piece of paper and communicate? And the second thing is, how do you make it happen?"

Motorola would create strategic objectives first. From there, it would develop goals and action plans, along with metrics to measure those goals. It took time, communication, and monitoring in order to create and maintain an effective organizational direction for Motorola and its team of more than 15,000 people.

IMEC: How much time does implementing Organizational Direction require?

RB: Generally, it takes more time the first year than it does the second year. It's like most things. The more you do it, the better you get at it.

IMEC: Who is responsible for Organizational Direction?

RB: The development of the strategy is the responsibility of the senior leaders. Most organizations have a process for developing and implementing strategy throughout the year, but the bulk of the development work happens in the last three months of the year. This is also when the communication process should come into play so that everyone understands the new strategic direction and what their individual roles in the strategy are as the new year starts.

We spent a lot of time developing this communication process. What did we want to communicate? Who did we want to make the communications? And who was the recipient?

IMEC: How did you communicate your organization's goals and action plans throughout the organization?

RB: Ideally, if you walked into our shop at Motorola and said to a person "How does your job contribute to the success of the organization, how does it play a part of the strategy?" 70% to 90% of our people should be able to tell you specifically how their job helps our organization be successful. And our associates' survey results were in that range.

We wanted to position it in such a way that the first line supervisor was knowledgeable about what was going on in the business because by and large, people want to hear things from their boss, and so we wanted that first line supervisor to be informed. We would prepare packages for them. We also gave them a way to ask questions where we could get them answers if something came up within their organizations.

IMEC: How did Motorola inform leaders to communicate the organizational strategy with their teams?

RB: We had a flow chart. This was a process map of who communicated what. This flow chart included answers to questions such as: What did the CEO of Motorola say? What did I say? What did people down the organization say? A thorough communication plan of your strategy is essential, especially for larger teams.

IMEC: Under your tenure, the Motorola two-way radio sector had 15,000 employees and was doing business in 170 different countries. Did you have processes in place for global team members?

RB: [The] leadership team had to create a process so that a person in another country could easily see how their work contributed to the strategy.

IMEC: While you were at Motorola, the leadership team surveyed every single employee to see who could explain exactly how their job contributed to the organization's overall strategy. Why was this so important to you?

RB: So they knew, when they came to work every day, this was how they were helping everybody be successful.

It's one thing to have a communication process, but is it effective? When we would be asking people, after we've done our communication for the week or the month or whatever, we'd say, "Okay, what did senior leaders say was important? Or what was the key message in this meeting?"

There would also be follow-up questions, such as, "Of the things they talked about, would you like them to do more or less, and of the things they didn't talk about, what would you like to see?"

The frequency with which employees were surveyed varied based on what and when communication was happening. If there was a town hall, Motorola may have people placed outside the doors of that meeting, ready to ask all attendees what their thoughts on the meeting were. If the feedback from our employees was not good, that either meant that Motorola leadership wasn't delivering the message well or they weren't discussing the right topic.

You're trying to figure out at the end of the day "Are we doing well? Is it effective? And the question is, 'how do you know?'"

IMEC: How important was customer input while aligning Organizational Direction to customer needs?

RB: It's important to continually get feedback from your customers because there are times when your customer's needs from your organization will change.

IMEC: How do you get meaningful customer feedback?

RB: In the development of the strategic plan, we're talking to customers. We're trying to get good input there. We would be riding with a lot of police officers, with a lot of fire departments; we'd be with the military. So that's the way we would understand the customer.

Besides ride-alongs, we also utilized surveys to get customer feedback.

IMEC: Who did the surveys?

RB: With the original survey distribution [done internally], Motorola was getting pretty high marks from customers, but then we decided to have an outside agency start calling customers to administer the survey. This led to more honest feedback from customers.

If you're accomplishing something like 90%, you don't want to just look at the 90%, you want to look at the 10%. What is the 10% that we aren't doing well? What can we learn there that will help us overall? We were trying to get very close to customers on a continual basis.

IMEC: Do you have an example survey question?

RB: Ask: "Here are the things we imagine we can do for you. What do you see that you would like us to accomplish for you in the next one year, in the next three years, in the next five years?"

IMEC: What other advice do you have for strategically-minded leaders?

RB: Know what do they [customers] say they do and what do they actually do. Mapping this behavior is all a part of strategic planning, as is the company's mission, vision, and values. The mission is what each piece of the organization does.

For example, what if your corporate mission is to provide the best two-way digital radio for the Chicago Police Department? How would each department or employee achieve that goal? They would each have different tasks or duties, which would be reflected in their department's mission statement.

Alongside the mission, a company also needs its vision statement. The vision is the lighthouse on the hill. Everybody can see it up there and that helps to align the vectors in terms of what they do. And then the strategy identifies the steps the organization takes to accomplish this mission and vision over time.

Mission and vision are high-level goals, but they don't explain how your employees are going to achieve those goals. The values are the way people act and the way people perform.

The core values define what is acceptable behavior, what's not, or what are the stated beliefs and the observed behaviors.

There were parts of this [the company's strategy, mission, and goals] that we wanted to communicate essentially on a daily basis, and then there are things we wanted to see on a weekly basis or a monthly basis or quarterly basis.

We [at Motorola] had a mantra, and it had three parts: customer intimacy, operational excellence, and technology superiority.

IMEC: Can you expand on what is customer intimacy?

RB: From a communication point of view, we were leading [our customers] and telling them this is what's possible... we believed that we needed to understand that part of their business better than they do. And so, we focused a lot on really being intimate with our customers and knowing specifically [how to develop what they need].

IMEC: How did you look at operational excellence and technology superiority?

RB: That's when we said we just want to be the best and, so, that was our effort of continuous improvement, and I know you see that in a lot of organizations where they're saying, "How do we get better at getting better?"

Regarding technology superiority, we were probably doing a thousand patents a year, so we wanted people to feel when they bought Motorola, when they bought our products, we were going to be with them over their lifetime and nobody could say they made a mistake by buying Motorola. IBM used to say nobody gets fired by buying from IBM, right? Well, we felt the same way about our business.

IMEC: How many goals should an organization have?

RB: You can't have twenty. What are the three or four most important initiatives that we are going to get done this next year, and what are the goals and action plans to make that happen.

FILE UNDER ORGANIZATIONAL SUCCESS

Documenting, communicating, monitoring, repeat. To some, planning for organizational success may seem daunting, but to Barnett, it is magic. Your organizational direction, when documented and available to all employees, allows everyone on your team to see how their work impacts the larger picture. It can have a huge impact on employee morale, and is one of the most important action steps for leadership teams.

Chapter 2

WORKFORCE AND CULTURE: COMPETING GLOBALLY STARTS AT HOME

Inspire your team to own it.

What does it take to build a truly remarkable team and a high-performing organization?

We've talked with many leaders in manufacturing, health care, education, and business to learn about the best practices and strategies they use to achieve performance excellence. Despite representing different industries, these organizations have taken some similar paths to performance excellence, and as such have overcome common challenges from which we can all learn.

One challenge that is all too familiar to manufacturers is the workforce crisis. With rising labor costs and a lack of skilled workers, manufacturers must take strategic actions to protect and build their greatest asset: people.

How do you engage and retain a high-performing workforce? How do you create a culture where people want to stay? What improvement strategies must you have in place to focus on enterprise excellence? How do you inspire people to be part of something bigger than themselves?

Most companies would be hard-pressed to improve in an area without a baseline. Organizational workforce and culture is another component of Baldrige that speaks to organizational success. Creating a workplace profile examines two main areas:

- **Workforce environment.** How do you build an effective and supportive workforce environment?
- **Workforce engagement.** How do you engage your workforce for retention and high performance?

In this chapter, we return to the "journey" afforded by the Baldrige challenge and explore your organizational success through the lens of your workforce. Then, we'll take a look at various roles within manufacturing, the path from hiring to retention, and the topic of workplace productivity across the organization. Our closing thoughts center around employee engagement and one of the biggest competitive advantages of all: creating a vibrant workplace culture. You will also meet Katherine Ramsey, Vice President Global Human Resources, and Kris Cuthbertson, Training and Operations Special Projects Manager, for G&W Electric, as they share G&W's

work culture and how diversity and inclusion has helped define the manufacturer.

Valuing people is a core concept behind IMEC's work, and it should be at the forefront of every leader's agenda. A successful organization values its workforce members and other stakeholders like customers, community members, suppliers and partners, and educational partners. Author Simon Sinek (otherwise known as the most famous person to underscore the importance of knowing your "why") said, "When people are financially invested, they want a return. When people are emotionally invested, they want to contribute."

Building a collaborative, engaged team will elevate your competitive position as a manufacturing company and help you grow.

THE SKILLS GAP DILEMMA

Many talk about the "skills gap" facing manufacturing. This problem is only partially true. Yes, there's a deficit in our skilled trades pipeline, and as employers, educators, and communities. We need to rally around the value of skilled trades and support the growth of this critical workforce, starting in junior high and beyond.

Yet, there's another gap that mid-market manufacturing is facing–the strategic gap. If you need to get strong talent into your organization, here are five ideas:

"Selling" your organization. You need to sell your organization, the role, and the value of being a part of your company to potential employees. Just like a potential customer, frame your sale around candidate interests and needs, starting with asking potential employees what they are looking for. Then develop a strategy to meet those needs. You are competing for talent.

Shore up your HR skill sets. Is your HR team flipping through resumes and looking for keywords, or evaluating candidates based on their skills? Your HR team needs a clear strategy to effectively assess organizational talent needs, and how they will assess candidates against the skills needed for the role. In speaking with a CEO of a construction company, he noted that they will only consider applicants with five specific previous titles in their work history. Titles vary from organization to organization, but skills are the real transferable value. Have a strategy to effectively evaluate and vet candidates skills.

Look outside your traditional recruitment channels and approaches. You have flooded the major internet job boards with job listings, but you're still getting little response, or lackluster candidates. *Why?* Firstly, you're likely not "selling" the position. Is it written in a way that talks about dry duty details and a canned overview of your company? Or does it communicate excitement and value to the potential employee (such as learning new skills, upward mobility, impact of their role)? Secondly, if you're getting little success online, go to where your candidates are. This can range from trade schools, to job fairs, to holding your own open house. Again, just like prospecting for customers, prospect for employees.

Look beyond your traditional competitors. Your competitors are not just other manufacturers. One vice president of operations at a regional manufacturing company noted that they struggle to secure talent, but they offer competitive salaries. While compared to other similar, smaller manufacturing companies in the area, the company's rates can be up to 12% more, but compared to the local Coscto (yes, Costco), they are almost 22% lower. In addition, they offer less flexibility in hours, time off and benefits. Even though you might believe a candidate is seeking a position in the manufacturing industry, they might be able to simply find a better paying, more flexible and higher growth job in another industry.

Re-examine your expectations. *The New York Times* reported the story of a manufacturer outside of Milwaukee that had twenty-five positions open for skilled workers. The manufacturer received more than 1,000 applications for positions. The company hired the twenty-five needed, but within a month fired fifteen of the employees because of their dissatisfaction with their wages and the company's work rules. The manufacturer's pay rate for a skilled technician with an associate degree was $15 per hour. By comparison, the local McDonald's was paying $14 per hour. Though not everyone is motivated by salary, understand what your expectations are as an employer, and if they are reasonable to the market. One manufacturing CEO said he was having a hard time finding welders–yet, he said he was looking for fifteen years experience for $14/hr, in addition to someone who would not call in sick, come to work early, and just "keep their head down and stay quiet." No doubt he will be hard-pressed to find talent.

In short, the recruitment and retention game has changed for manufacturing. In this competitive environment, it may be difficult to pay the wages and benefits necessary to attract individuals with the education and skills desired; however, that does not mean that those skills are missing. Fill the strategic gap if you want to truly overcome today's workforce challenge.

IMEC wishes to thank Andrea Belk Olsen, CEO of Pragmadik, for contributing to Made in Illinois.

WIN-WIN COLLABORATION IS A SKILL FOR FRONTLINE SUPERVISORS

Collaboration sometimes involves working with people who have different views than your own. Frontline supervisors who master this skill recognize differences and confidently state their own position while also honoring the opposing viewpoint in order to arrive at the best possible solution.

What does an environment with exceptional collaboration look like? Frontline workers are listened to with respect. Their opinions are taken into consideration. The trust level on the plant floor is high. Consider these points:

Mastering conflict resolution. Conflicts will arise, even within the best teams. Communication is key to resolving these conflicts, but you also want to make sure direct reports to the frontline supervisor feel comfortable enough to bring differences of opinion to the forefront. Consider conflict resolution training and sharing personality and behavioral assessment results.

Implementing effective motivation. Not every employee is the same, and therefore they are motivated by different factors. As a frontline supervisor, part of your responsibility is to understand each of your employees and find their underlying motivations. These motivations aren't always what you think.

Proper incentive plans for each employee are only one step. It is important to incentivize your employees for the right behaviors and make sure your employees come to work every day knowing exactly how they contribute to the company's mission.

Employees want more than just good pay. They want to know that their work is valued, that their voices are heard, that their work environments are safe, and more, depending on the specific employee.

One way to understand employees is through an employee engagement survey, a longer form survey that measures their happiness and how they feel valued within the organization.

Maximizing high performance coaching. Challenging people while bringing out their best ties in with motivation. How you coach employees varies per employee. Frontline supervisors should work with employees to make sure they are poised for success. When employees are successful, the company is successful.

Do they have the right tools? Do they need more training? Is their workspace set up for their individual optimal performance? Can waste be reduced in their daily routine?

Leadership building. There are many books written around leadership and, while space does not permit us to discuss the topic in-depth, the big takeaway is for you to enhance the frontline supervisor's leadership training through continuous learning. Recognize capable leaders within your team, and set them up for success. Developing leadership building skills might include leadership courses, career development plans, mastering delegation skills, emotional intelligence training, or conversations around the company's mission and business strategy.

Implementing practical training. How are you currently training your staff? Do you only train new employees, or do you offer continuous learning? Is your training redundant or outdated? Is it longer or shorter than it should be? Can portions of it be moved to virtual? Are you standardizing your training, or do you have custom training per job role? Later in this chapter, we will discuss proven training methods to get the most out of your team.

Frontline supervisors have a huge responsibility to create a positive, success-driven culture that directly impacts profitability, innovation, and employee morale. Recognize this special role and invest in their success.

FRONTLINE WORKERS: THE VALUE ADDING ASSOCIATE

"Production" frontline associates deserve appreciation for providing us with goods and services we need. It is easy to take the contribution of frontline workers for granted. One way to respect their time and value is to understand the "famous" eight wastes.

- Defects
- Overproduction
- Waiting
- Non-utilization of people and talent
- Transportation
- Inventory
- Motion
- Excess processing

As you can see, these spell out DOWNTIME. Of these, not allowing people to use their full potential is probably the single biggest waste. Companies where the culture does not fully respect the human potential are not ready for a meaningful, sustained journey to excellence. It is simply not going to happen. In fact, lack of respect is likely to stall the journey. And it has. We've seen countless companies starting on their lean or excellence journey that don't finish because the culture of respect, particularly for the frontline associate, is missing.

Those that have sustained it, notably Toyota, have made human development the core of their culture. Idea generation and promotion, designing one's own work process, empowerment to solve problems, among others, are the hallmarks of lean systems such as the Toyota Production System (TPS). TPS has been wildly successful for over fifty years and across the globe in distinctly different local cultures. Why? Respect for people, especially toward those at the frontline, is an integral part of such systems. This respect is not just about being superficially nice (cue the occasional "bagel day") or saying kind words. It is a deep-rooted culture of humility, recognizing the following two points:

- Frontline work is indeed what customers are willing to pay for. It is value-added work.
- Frontline associates have expert knowledge about the processes they run.

Frontline operators in manufacturing are value adders. Can we assist the value adders in providing even more value? This is a winning attitude. When it is the pervasive attitude in an organization, it is a winning culture.

THE INTERVIEW THAT GIVES PEOPLE A REASON TO STAY

How can you truly make each individual employee a priority? Consider stay interviews.

Stay interviews are one-on-one conversations conducted by a leader, usually an employee's direct manager or supervisor. They are used to reveal what is important to each employee and how their aspirations can be fulfilled. Having meaningful conversations that aren't about topics like performance or attendance builds trust and ultimately retains key players. In fact, these interviews are healthy for a company regardless of whether you believe an employee is planning to leave or not.

As you think about creating a process and developing information for stay interviews, consider the following points:

- Introduce the topic to the workforce. Go over things such as the purpose, importance, and expectations.
- Inform individuals to be prepared to bring one to three topics that they would like to discuss.
- Focus on areas that are important to the person with whom you are speaking.
- Create a handful of open-ended questions and be prepared for follow-up conversation.
    - *Sample question: "When you come to work each day, what do you look forward to?"*
- Confirm a neutral area in which each employee feels comfortable having this discussion.

With high-level insight about the planning stage, you are ready to move to the next step, which is acquiring the skills needed to conduct interviews.

Once you've investigated the idea to implement stay interviews, the next step is to explore the types of skills you will need as an interviewer. Being a successful leader includes holding meaningful conversations–a skill that requires effort and practice. The following are three key skills that will make your stay interviews a success.

Build trust. At a granular level, building trust fosters open communication, allows for reliability and consistency, as well as boosts confidence in others. All of these will begin to surface when a leader's actions and words align.

Actively listen. During a stay interview, it is key to be silent while the employee is speaking. This aids in receptivity and a better understanding of the information they are sharing. In addition, the other part of actively listening is to demonstrate what was heard. To check for understanding, follow up with something such as, "If I understand you correctly, you are saying..." or "What I think I'm hearing is . . ."

Investigate information. During the conversation, the employee might share being "so stressed" or even "super busy." Rather than dismissing it, probe further. Ask additional open-ended questions like: "Can you share an example of . . ." or "Tell me when and where you felt this recently . . .". Find out why they feel the way they do. You might be surprised at what you learn. An answer like: "I'm not appreciated on the team," for example, could give way to actionable change. Ultimately, seek to understand the employee's full perspective.

As you strengthen the necessary skills, you will conduct effective interviews as well as create the components needed for an impactful stay plan. Then, you will be well positioned as an employer of choice.

THE REAL VALUE OF TRAINING WITHIN INDUSTRY

Training Within Industry (TWI) is a proven job training methodology that has been implemented successfully by companies for decades (not to be confused with Urban Dictionary's definition of "texting while intoxicated"). Basically, TWI was developed during WWII as part of the War Manpower Commission as a way to ready plants with skilled personnel in high demand industries. More than 1.6 million people working in 16,500 plants received certification, with TWI later becoming the foundation for the Toyota Production System.[17]

What prompts a manufacturer to employ TWI? When you shift production to a different product to meet customer needs or reassign team members to other jobs in the face of workforce reduction. As we've seen, the Defense Production Act may require a company to shift production to a different product and therefore need to rapidly train team members. Some companies are hiring so rapidly that they interview a person, hire them on the spot, and the person is working on the job the same day. These new team members require training on everything from safety and time–keeping to actual daily tasks.

While there are different steps to TWI, understanding the why behind whatever we are

doing greatly improves retention. Author John C. Maxwell puts it this way: "Find your why and you'll find your way."

Job instruction method, a TWI method, allows a person to quickly remember to do a job, correctly, safely, and conscientiously. Job Instruction allows you to achieve rapid learning by following four steps to training preparation. Then, once you are ready, you follow another four steps to transfer the knowledge to the trainee.

Four Steps to Prepare to Train:

Have a training timetable. Basically, this means you need a plan on *who* is going to be trained, on *what* task, and by *when.* This may seem simple, but consider a new hire, or someone who is moved to a different job. Do you know exactly what tasks they will be trained on, and in which order? Or do they just "shadow" another employee and learn to do what "they" do?

Break down the job. Once you know what tasks someone is going to be trained on, you need to define the best way to perform the task. Do you have standard operating procedures, work instructions, visual aids, etc.? The task should be broken into three areas: essential steps of the job, *key points* to the job, and the reason *why* we do it a certain way.

Have everything ready. Again, this may seem simple. However, if the trainer is not prepared to train, then training can become confusing and more difficult for the new hire to quickly learn. Consider creating checklists, a frequently asked questions handout, and checking trainer availability.

Arrange the worksite. For the trainee to quickly learn and complete their tasks, the training should be conducted in the actual working environment when possible.

Once you have completed the four steps in preparation to train, you are now ready to transfer the information to the new hires or trainees.

4-Step Job Instruction Method for Training:

Prepare the worker. The trainer should put the employee at ease. The new hire may be nervous or worried about learning a new task. The trainer should clearly explain the task and find out the experience level of the employee. This will help ensure the task they are about to learn is within his or her capabilities. Next, explain why the task is important, and its impact on the rest of the organization or the final product.

Present the operation three times. First demonstrate the task and explain the important steps. The second time, demonstrate again, review the important steps, and add the key points. Lastly, demonstrate, review the important steps, key points, and reasons it is being done that specific way.

Have the employee perform the task at least four times. The first time, just have the worker complete the task and correct any errors. The second time, have them complete the task while telling you what the important steps are. The third time, the worker should complete the task, tell you the important steps, and key points. The fourth time, the employee completes the task, explains the important steps, key points, and reasons why it's important to the company or product.

Follow up. Once the trainer is convinced the employee knows how to complete the task, the worker will need a few more directions from the trainer, like who to go to for help, when to expect check-ins from the trainer, and when coaching will be completed. Trainers should encourage trainees to ask questions throughout the coaching process.

Now, more than ever, with the quick changes in our work, we need a method to quickly train our team members so they can quickly learn to complete a task correctly, safety, and understand why they are doing it.

TEN MYTHS ABOUT TRAINING WITHIN INDUSTRY

Given the challenges of today's skills gap, systematic approaches to train and retrain staff pays dividends. Yet, we hear plenty of myths about TWI that hold manufacturers back from operating at peak performance. Let's take a look.

1. **It takes too long to train this way.** Trainers often think that because we repeat the instruction multiple times and have the employee try the performance multiple times, that training takes too long. They often think it is easier to just show the employee once, have them do it once, and then leave them to fend for themselves. It may seem like this saves time but think of all the quality problems that are caused by poor training and the lack of productivity. Although you may save time on the interaction you have with the employee, in fact, you spend more time correcting problems, answering questions, and being frustrated because that worker just doesn't get it.

2. **The method is just too repetitive.** It probably is too repetitive for you, the trainer, because you know the job so well. But this isn't about you, it is about the employee who is most likely just seeing the job or paying attention to the way it is done for the first time. So, you're instructing three times and the employee repeating and executing it four times is not repetitive to that individual at all. This is all about the worker.
3. **This method doesn't work for jobs that take a long time to do.** This method still works to train people on jobs that have many steps. Evaluate the job and see how it can be broken down into smaller chunks. Quite frequently there are natural rest points that allow you to train small pieces of the job. This may require that you only train and allow the worker to learn a small piece and then you do the rest of the job to keep production moving. We can only learn so much at one time. Trying to cram too much in at once can make it harder–not faster–for us to learn the jobs.
4. **I can't give just brief descriptions of what I am doing; I need to go into much greater detail.** Eventually you will want to go into more detail about the job and the procedure; right now, you want the trainee to learn how to do the job correctly, safely, and conscientiously. Refer them to operating procedures and visual work tools when they are available and avoid overwhelming people with more information than they need at one time.

5. **I already know the worker I am training so I don't have to prepare the worker.** Preparing the worker means making sure they are ready to be trained and knowing their skill level. This allows you to be prepared. For instance, if you are going to teach someone how to measure a part, the employee will need to know how to use the measuring device. Thus, this may be where you start the training rather than jumping to how to measure the specific part. Put the employee in a position where the job can be easily viewed, setting them up for success.
6. **I only have "important steps" and no key points so I should only have to show the employee once.** First, make sure you really don't have any key points. Are there things that would make or break the job, injure the worker, or make the job easier to do? If not, you still need to show-and-tell the job to the employee at least three times. Repetition is important. That's the way we learn. It's like doing only one addition problem before you moved on to subtraction when you were in school (sorry to bring up any bad math memories).
7. **The worker did the job correctly the first time, so I know he knows the job and I don't have to have him repeat it three more times.** The employee often can do the job correctly the first time; however, you still don't know if the task is fully understood. It is important that you have the employee show you and tell you about the job at least three more times. You

can't know what the employee is thinking, seeing, or hearing. You must have the employee say it aloud to validate the learning.

8. **The worker told me all the steps, key points, and reasons and demonstrated their performance. They were still making mistakes, but did the task four times so I can leave them on their own.** Remember to continue until you know they know the job. Just because they demonstrated four times, doesn't necessarily mean they are ready to be on their own. Continue to correct their mistakes and make sure that they know it well enough that they will produce good parts and won't get hurt. Follow up is also a necessity. Check back on them frequently while they are learning. Also, make sure someone is available nearby to help them. (By the way, don't forget to make sure the person nearby does the work to the same standard process.)
9. **I need to give reasons for all the steps otherwise the employee won't understand how difficult this job really is.** Emphasize important details and make sure the employee understands why the job needs to be done this certain way. A step is a step. This is what is done to move the job forward. Establishing these steps as THE way to do the job puts you on the path to establishing standard work.
10. **There is too much up front planning in TWI. It's a lot easier if I leave the employee to just figure out whatever is going on that day.** It may be easier for

> you, but this puts a tremendous burden on the worker. Our brains like structure and clarity. No matter how smart the employee is, just having them figure out the job with no plan or organized process can be very frustrating. They may be left feeling like they will never learn, have no idea how to ensure good quality, or how to keep safe. The four-step TWI Job Instruction process allows you to prepare yourself to do the best job training so others can quickly learn to do a job correctly, safely and conscientiously.

The big takeaway: if the employee hasn't learned, the instructor hasn't taught to their greatest potential.

SEEING THE BRILLIANT LUSTRE OF YOUR EMPLOYEE'S GREATEST POTENTIAL

How do you solve the ongoing shortage of skilled employees in manufacturing? The first order of business is to highly engage the team you have, and the second order of business is to create a highly-skilled, energized team of producers. Enter the diamond metaphor.

Just like a diamond, people have many different facets.

So how do you polish and "set" your "diamond" in settings that will bring out their brilliance? Where do you first mine the diamonds in your company? Mining and sorting diamonds is a lengthy process, and you must look at each "diamond" individually to see how to get the most from it. Why do we take the time to sort these diamonds? Is it because of the value they bring when they are polished? Is the extensive time we take worth the effort? All good questions around diamonds and the answers to the questions are unequivocally, yes.

Shouldn't this be the same for our employees? You can bring out their brilliance in so many ways, and training is one of them.

- Start with engagement surveys to identify the gaps between company values and employee values.
- Understand what the true needs are and align them.
- Use a DiSC personality profile (a personal assessment tool that helps improve working relationships by understanding individual personalities; DiSC stands for dominance, influence, steadiness, conscientiousness) to understand how your employees think and to find out what energizes them.
- Implement a leadership needs analysis to see their "clarity" and to "shape" them into greater brilliance.
- Use the TWI methodology (the Training Within Industry approach we talked about earlier) to cross-train teams and add to their value.

COMMON THEMES FROM IMEC'S EMPLOYEE ENGAGEMENT PULSE SURVEYS

You can improve workplace and company culture (isn't it a great feeling to love where you work?) through insight from employees. One vetted tool that focuses on engagement levels is a pulse survey, a brief survey that captures and measures employee feedback on a real-time basis. This allows leadership to more easily make adjustments in the workplace. Pulse surveys, typically completed in under five minutes, are much shorter than employee engagement surveys.

To help leaders obtain this information, IMEC created a pulse survey to assist companies to identify what employees are going through. The brief survey consists of questions that seek both qualitative information (what employees are saying today) as well as quantitative information (what the numbers tell us is going on). Administer this survey electronically and expect answers back within one to two days.

After conducting multiple pulse surveys, IMEC has found several common themes among them. In addition to creating a safer work environment, which is at the forefront of everyone's mind, the following themes race to the top:

- Improving communication
- Creating and maintaining an atmosphere of trust
- Providing meaningful recognition

Improving Communication

With the US unemployment rate surpassing forty million at the time of publishing, employees have indicated that they are seeking more transparent communication from leaders. They are seeking both formal and informal types of communication.

For example, when thinking of sharing information in a formal setting, how and when information is conveyed become critical. One production employee indicated that the company can show support by "keeping good communication as to what is happening or expected to happen in the near future." Another individual said, "Communication that is critical needs to be shared and understood at every level of the company." Leaders have been reporting that they communicate via email. Although updates are being shared, in many cases, production personnel are still seeking that face-to-face interaction. This allows for questions to be answered as well as for a working relationship to flourish.

Leaders must also make it a point to keep in contact on an individual basis, more informally. The pulse survey indicated that 76% either agree or strongly agree that their manager is regularly checking in with how they are doing (not just work-related). A frontline worker stated, "Visit and talk to individuals one-on-one. Without a formalized setting, one can truly then get a feeling of concerns, etc. Walk-arounds and informal sit-downs would instill a great way to build that stronger connection." This recurring topic shows how important it is for employees to have a personal connection with leaders.

Creating and Maintaining an Atmosphere of Trust

Something that is just as important as providing transparent communication is creating and maintaining an atmosphere of trust. As mentioned earlier, trust is a main factor of determining organizational success, and the need for it came through loud and clear as a theme in the survey findings. Although many leaders know this, trust doesn't develop overnight. It is critical for your workforce to remain united and resilient. The secret sauce for that to happen successfully is trust.

As the saying goes, "People don't quit a job, they quit a boss." In fact, Gallup estimates "[an employee's relationship with their] manager accounts for at least 70% of variance in employee engagement scores across business units."[18] Statements like this show just how influential managers are. One frontline worker who responded to our survey said, "The workers have lost faith and trust in the management and that causes lack of performance and attendance. The management needs to find out how to regain trust." IMEC's pulse survey indicates that regardless of company size or product being made, trust is essential. It is needed to increase hope, morale, relationships, productivity, and engagement levels.

Providing Meaningful Recognition

Employees are seeking genuine recognition from leaders. In fact, 72% of employees agree or strongly agree that their supervisor provides positive recognition. Then, when focusing on management, the level of agreement drops to 64%.

Many know that for recognition to have purpose, it goes beyond a pizza party or bringing in donuts. Yes, those are nice things to do. However, consider how effective they are when seeking desired, longer-term outcomes.

When IMEC surveyed a remote department, one employee stated, "I do believe that we all need some form of happiness. Virtual high fives or thank you notes to be passed around . . . anything to bring smiles." People seek quick, yet thoughtful suggestions for recognizing a job well done. Virtual employees continue to seek human relationship building.

People are seeking positive recognition. Whether

workloads have been inconsistent or at an all-time high, leaders must pause and take a step back with the team to see what they have accomplished to date. When asked, "How can the company support you at this time?" one employee indicated: "Keep up the community spirit, recognize people for their unique talents." Taking recognition a step further, one frontline employee wrote: "The factory workers are the bread and butter of the company. If they aren't there, no one has a job." It was a humbling statement describing how some positions might go unnoticed. A great starting point is to recognize individuals in a timely and personable manner. Every job is critical to the success of an organization.

FACILITATING A SUCCESSFUL EMPLOYEE ENGAGEMENT SURVEY: FIVE LESSONS ON LEVERAGING ORGANIZATIONAL SUCCESS

Are you planning to implement, or have you recently deployed, an employee engagement survey to your workforce? Are you unsure of what to do next or are seeing little to no improvement? As you implement and evaluate engagement levels, there are many hurdles and successes. Here are five lessons for leveraging organizational success through an employee engagement survey:

Leadership needs to be fully on board and supportive of improving engagement levels. Ask leadership why they want to focus on engagement within the workplace. You might hear "HR wants to measure it" or "a millennial told me to." These responses might trigger a deeper dive. The organizations that succeed with implementing an employee engagement survey have leadership personnel who are passionate about the company, their workforce, and the bottom line. They are strategic thinkers who are ready to embrace the perceptions of all team members.

Designate an internal champion to project manage action items that surface from the survey responses. An internal champion is crucial when improving engagement levels within an organization. This individual will take part in developing a project charter, finalizing action items, and project management beyond the survey. When this team member is present, you may see an increase in action items being worked toward and successfully completed, an organized approach when working with quantitative and qualitative data, and a supportive and transparent workplace.

Communicate effectively when focusing on engagement levels. Communication plans are pertinent and critical during the facilitation of the survey process and beyond. With that said, leaders and other influential individuals need to make sure communication is present. More specifically, communication needs to begin prior to the survey, during the day of facilitation, directly after, when sharing results, and throughout the time action items are being created and implemented. These points of communication allow the workforce to better understand the reason as to why this topic is being focused on, the role people have with this process, and what changes will be seen.

Don't get "hung up" on the quantitative data. You need to create a method of obtaining and taking action with qualitative data. Throughout the years of focusing on engagement, some companies get hung up on the quantitative data from employee engagement surveys. Yes, this data is important to focus on when improving engagement levels. However, don't have blinders on and ignore what employees are saying. In the survey process, make sure that workforce personnel take part in focus groups. From conversations with these groups, there is important, if not even more fruitful, information collected than just numbers.

Do something with the survey results. Through working with companies, and through research, there is excitement and drive when receiving the survey and focus group results. However, that drive will sometimes diminish. Whether during the result meeting or throughout the initial stages of working on action items, some leaders (or champions) lose motivation when attempting to make progress with engagement results. Yes, other business operations may be detrimental. However, without your workforce, how can you exist?

Many key players wear multiple hats, and it's totally fine to ask for assistance with the employee engagement process. In fact, when you involve a voluntary group of people on an employee engagement committee, there is great energy moving forward with engagement results.

THREE FOUNDATIONAL REASONS PRODUCTIVITY LEVELS VARY

In many cases, the demand from our work has increased, our families continue to need our love and support, and we as individuals need to make sure that we are mentally focused. With that said, there are certain times that our productivity habits can fluctuate. The following are three common areas in which productivity habits can vary, as well as takeaways to increase efficiency.

1. **Work environment.** From cleanliness to room temperature, a work environment can be detrimental to how productive someone can be. Those who enjoy their workspace will be more productive, engaged, happy, and healthy. Consider these tips when reevaluating a work environment:

- Continuously make changes to evolve you and your work output.
- Have a layout that is realistic and accommodates your needs in order to thrive with resources and tools readily available.
- Focus on subtle factors like lighting, noise level, and ideal temperature.

2. Job Security. It is natural for people to crave the need to experience predictability and control in their lives. If this doesn't happen, anxiety can grow within. According to American psychologist Abraham Maslow, there is a hierarchy of needs that people seek out to obtain human motivation.[19] One of those needs is safety. For a person to feel safe and secure in life, emotional security and financial security must surface.

Regardless if your company has experienced some type of failure, or you missed your objectives, one can still manage and continue to grow. The following are a few takeaways to consider:

- Have a transparent discussion with the rest of the workforce to provide and seek relevant updates.
- Take a deep breath and be able to adjust to the new normal.
- Seek and welcome feedback from people both inside and outside of work.

3. Maintaining Working Relationships. Establishing, maintaining, and growing working relationships is key to how productive someone can be. On average, people spend more than 90,000 hours at work during their lifetime. To know there is a significant amount of time spent with your colleagues, you want to make the most of it. Here are some ways to build working relationships:

- Develop mutual accountability and a clear understanding of work responsibilities with colleagues.
- Learn to see things differently and put yourself in someone else's shoes to gain a better understanding of that person's perspective.
- Maintain a balance between meeting business objectives, but also allow time to focus on personal needs of others, such as incorporating esteem and empathy, encouraging involvement, sharing ideas, and lending support.

A TOP-DOWN APPROACH TO A SAFE WORK ENVIRONMENT

When safety is treated at the same level of importance as productivity, cost savings, and quality, then companies prevent more injuries on the manufacturing floor. How can you incorporate safety in your daily work interactions?

It is up to supervisors and managers to ensure a safe work environment. When leaders enforce safety rules and empower employees to maintain safety standards, injuries can be prevented. A safer work environment is achievable when you employ the following:

- Create a "safety first" environment, where safety is as important as your company's other values.
- Incorporate daily walks where you observe, correct, and coach.
- Use all your senses to identify potential risks, address them with your employees, and teach them how to mitigate those risks and avoid injuries.
- Be proactive and enforce a Personal Protection Equipment (PPE) policy at all times (start with yourself).
- Praise and thank your employees when using best PPE practices and address any areas for improvement in a coaching manner.
- When you sense something is not right, address it immediately with your employee (do not wait because managers have an obligation to incorporate safety conversations daily).

An injured employee impacts not only themselves and their families, but also their coworkers, supervisors, and the organization as a whole. Productivity decelerates, quality becomes questionable, the organization gets hit with a big medical bill–and, yet, all these things can be prevented. By integrating safety in your organization, there is a much higher chance to increase the quality of your products and services, as well as productivity, by keeping morale high and employees motivated.

Keep in mind that a company's culture will not change if you are not starting with a top-down approach; it starts with you, the leader. Make a joint effort to incorporate safety behaviors and principles in our daily interactions with employees.

CARING: ONE PATH TO IMPROVING WORKPLACE SAFETY

Safety training and policies are commonly used tools to encourage a safety culture. However, these practices alone will not be enough. Engaging employees and showing them that they are valued also creates a safer workplace.

When workers feel cared for, respected, and appreciated, they are far more likely to be committed to a safe workplace. They will also pay it forward by caring for other workers and helping them avoid dangers. The SHRM Foundation studied employee engagement for beverage giant Molson Coors and found "engaged employees were five times less likely than non-engaged employees to have a safety incident and seven times less likely to have a lost-time safety incident. The company was able to save $1,721,760 in safety costs, just by strengthening their commitment to employee engagement."[20]

Leaders and managers send many subtle signals to their employees every day that indicate to workers whether they really care about them. A picture is worth a thousand words. Have you looked around to see the conditions you provide your employees? For example, a clean, functioning, and nicely decorated break room or restroom demonstrates a company's commitment to employees. Nicked up walls or a broken microwave sends quite a different message.

Here are six recommendations to put on your to-do list to help create a more caring environment, thus leading to a safer workplace:

1. **Clean surfaces with sanitizer or disinfectant regularly.** Keep countertops, tables, and work surfaces clean and our employees healthy.
2. **Spruce up bathrooms and other common areas**. A clean coat of paint with an updated color on the walls can make a big difference in employees' moods and satisfaction. Give common areas a makeover so people can relax and feel comfortable while on break.
3. **Keep restrooms clean.** An interesting way to gauge workplace safety culture is by observing the cleanliness of restrooms and break areas. These areas should be clean and well-stocked with supplies. Also, be sure these areas are well lit and presentable.

4. **Repair or replace broken furniture, appliances, and plumbing.** If a chair is broken, it shouldn't be used. Safety doesn't just apply to the shop floor and office; workers should be safe in every part of the building. Worn cords on appliances? A refrigerator that doesn't stay cold? Plumbing that is leaking? Fix or replace them. Safety is for everyone, everywhere.
5. **Provide clean hand washing areas that are well-stocked with dryers, soap, and paper towels.** Regularly emphasize good handwashing in your safety talks, one-on-one conversations, through signage, and by your own personal example. Not only does good hand hygiene prevent exposure to germs, it also prevents ingestion of hazardous chemicals and dirt that may get on employees' hands while performing their work.
6. **Establish a workplace cleanliness policy.** You don't have to do it all. You can distribute responsibilities throughout your workforce. However, as a leader you must make sure you adhere to the policy you establish.

REMOTE WORKERS AND THE FUTURE OF WORKING FROM ANYWHERE

At IMEC, we periodically host roundtable discussions with up to eight manufacturers hailing from diverse industries and geographic locations. Through these small group conversations, participants share their urgent challenges and ideas with one another. Repeatedly, participants have expressed the need to better manage a virtual workforce. For leaders, addressing concerns from workers allows you to be better prepared to discuss topics and create a culture where people feel understood and valued.

Let's start with a clear definition. Remote workers are those who are geographically dispersed, functionally diverse, and who rely on a variety of interactive technologies such as email, text, chat, webcams, and video conferencing to meet performance objectives. Typically, they work from home-based offices (not an easy feat for those short on space or long on distractions!) and are often juggling family responsibilities alongside work requirements. Virtual work is nothing new. It came on the business scene more than twenty years ago when technology, global competition, and the need for just-in-time customer service became business imperatives. In 2020, however, the number of remote workers virtually exploded overnight due to the pandemic.

In several discussions, we explored the chief concerns felt by remote workers. Here's a fresh look at remote work through the eyes of your peers:

- How long will I have to work from home?

- I like working from home; what if my company requires me to go back?
- Does my supervisor trust that I am working? Do my coworkers trust that I am working?
- Why are they piling on more work just because I'm working from home? I'm busier than ever.
- With limited places to go this year, we probably won't even take a vacation. So, does every day become a workday?
- How do I set the necessary boundaries between work, family, and social life?

The following are factors to help you successfully manage your new crop of virtual workers. By combining *technology* with *trust*, you'll have a winning combination.

Remote workers *rely* on technology. Unlike their brick-and-mortar colleagues who can get answers by walking down the hallway, virtual workers depend on technology for daily information, sales trends, project reports, and even social interactions with coworkers and management. Evaluate the technology provided for their use by asking these questions.

- What hardware will they use?
- What software functionality do they *truly need*?
- Do they have reliable internet connections with broad bandwidth capable of downloading large files?
- What video conferencing and software systems are available?

- How will we train people on new platforms?
- What channel of communication will we use to share ideas?
- Has our workflow process changed and, if so, how?

Equip remote workers with cameras and reliable audio connections. Many laptops have solid, built-in capabilities. During meetings, ask everyone to come "on camera" and if possible "off mute." This sets the stage for a more natural form of communication. The camera feature allows us to read body language, thus reducing misunderstandings. Seeing people also improves trust. Understandably, ask workers to use the mute feature when Coco the chihuahua starts barking or Sweet Pea the pug pounces on her squeaky toy (one clear benefit of cats is their more demure vocal range!).

Don't be afraid to use technology for problem-solving and brainstorming—cameras and annotation features can actually facilitate these conversations. Once you get used to using the chat box, polls, and annotation features, they will become a natural addition to every virtual meeting.

Provide not only the technology the worker needs, but also the training to use that technology. A few hours of focused work with someone who knows the systems relatively well can help answer questions and make employees feel more confident.

Overall, keep it simple. Be mindful of people's skills and their tolerance levels for troubleshooting or, minimally, directing them on who to call for technical help.

What Leaders Can Do

Now let's take a look at remote work through the lens of leaders.

As roundtable participants have shared, virtual workers who perform work anytime and at any place can be challenging to manage in traditional ways. Here are questions top of mind for leaders.

- How can I determine if the worker is doing a good job?
- How are supervisors maintaining interactions and connections with remote workers?
- Is that worker really working? How productive are they?
- Should I up my requests so that I'm assured that the worker is working?
- What boundaries should I impose?

The number one concern among leaders who manage remote workers is whether these workers will be as productive as they are in the building. Of course, the answer varies by individual. The key here is, don't take the wait-and-see approach. A blog on the subject by TechRepublic calls for leaders to set clear expectations and not pile on the extra work for employees just because they are remote. Actually, these are great points to remember whether we're managing virtually or in-person.[21] By focusing on outcomes and project work completed on time, you can instill a sense of independence and trust among remote workers. Experts recommend that leaders allow and actually encourage a great deal of autonomy and independent decision-making. The old top-down "do it because I said so" form of leadership will not work here. (Incidentally, it never was sustainable, even when we were face-to-face, so this is a great practice for the long haul.)

Do make a conscious effort to improve the speed of your response time. When workers are face-to-face, they can get answers to questions relatively quickly. Remote workers, on the other hand, might wait hours for a simple response. Share with employees and agree on a communications protocol. For example, you may be processing hundreds of emails every day. If a question needs your urgent attention, agree with remote workers that they will call or text you to alert you to the time-sensitive request or put "URGENT" in the subject line.

Continue with daily meetings. Have a quick, daily check-in, even if the employee is not physically in the office (often called "stand-up" meetings because they are super quick and avoid the longer conversations that come by way of sitting down).

When multiple immediate needs are calling for our attention, and tomorrow is still unclear, it's easy to lose sight of the organizational culture and strategic direction. How are you sharing the broader goals and values of the organization, and making sure all stay-at-home workers continue to keep your company mission in sight?

Here are a few last tips:

- Talk to work-at-home employees at least once a week to find out how it is going for them, personally and professionally (this builds trust).
- Continue to recognize remote workers for input and encourage others on the team to seek them out for their experience and ideas.
- Make sure virtual workers feel involved and connected, and keep everyone focused with routine updates,

In summary, check your technology, check in frequently, and check your focus on where you're headed as an organization. Working from home can help save money, improve employee engagement, reduce turnover, and provide higher levels of job satisfaction. Use remote opportunities to increase workers' sense of independence, while you promote a healthier work-life balance. That's a safe practice that bodes well for all of us, not only now, but into the future.

UPSKILLING YOUR TEAM IN VIRTUAL CLASSROOMS THAT INSPIRE REAL LEARNING

Training and upskilling workers today requires great leaps in creativity, innovation, and change management along with strong practices of human interaction. In other words, how we learn has taken a gigantic leap forward.

Virtual learning, once an experimental option for high tech offices, has become a new reality.

Employee retention and satisfaction continue to be

linked with learning opportunities, requiring manufacturers to find innovative ways to not only cross-train to help get products out the door, but also to use training as a way to show employees how much the organization values them.

We get it. As a training provider, remote learning is a big priority at IMEC. Many manufacturing companies have been either unable or reluctant to allow outsiders to enter their facilities during the pandemic, and, if they have, the requirements for socially distanced classrooms and teaching behind a face mask provide special challenges to even the most experienced classroom facilitator.

In a poll among IMEC trainers, we agreed that we miss employees' body language and eye contact to tell us if they are getting the message. We miss the small signals that tell us they need a break. We miss impromptu questions and ideas as the group learns a new topic and begins to, in the moment, mentally apply the lesson and ask questions.

Fortunately, virtual learning platforms can help. They provide tools like annotation, polling, and chat rooms. They give us immediate access into people's homes-turned-offices (with a few barks or meows in the background). What they don't give us are assurances that everyone is following along, no one is drifting off to multi-task, and learners are motivated to put the new learning into practice.

Here are simple tips to assure that any type of virtual learning you undertake has an opportunity for success:

- Keep the learning bite-sized
- Provide opportunities for immediate application
- Follow up, follow up, follow up

Keep the Learning Bite-Sized

Some highly paid consultants have purchased expensive cameras and performed extensive lighting do-overs in their kitchens so that they can deliver the exact same eight hours of learning they used to via webcam. Long, drawn out lectures might be a great sleep remedy, but don't often translate well into virtual. Think of the old adage: first, consider your audience. Virtual fatigue is real, and anyone who has endured even two hours of webinar material understands. Consider instead, breaking the learning into small chunks.

Micro-courses are short bursts of learning lasting no longer than ten to twenty minutes. They include key ingredients for sustaining a learner's attention: interactive quizzes, multiple choice options, and provocative case studies. Because they are short, bite-sized nuggets, they don't exhaust the learner, but they provide valuable insights to help learners move forward.

If you've ever watched a TED talk, you'll notice the maximum length is eighteen minutes (there are so many good ones; you should check them out) with many speeches clocking in at around nine minutes. Neuroscience explains why. The longer the learning duration, the more "cognitive backlog" we accumulate.[22] As the name implies, a backlog of facts and information can literally "weigh" down our minds.

Identify Ways to Immediately Apply the Learning

When learners immediately apply what they've learned, the chances of that learning "sticking" is greatly increased. This is where some pre-planning comes into play. Before you even select the training topic, answer this question, "As a result of this learning, the trainee will be able to . . . ?" Try to keep your scope to no more than three to five bullet points–these become the learning objectives and can help you select the type of training that is best suited.

Another great question you can ask as you plan is, "What will success look like?"

When you know where you're headed, you can begin to think of real-world practical experiences you want the learner to be able to do as a result of the training. For example, if learners need to provide better customer service, you can ask that they participate in a short, virtual learning module, then shadow an all-star performer and observe how that person handles difficult customer situations. Shadowing in a virtual world might mean inviting the learner to a video meeting or looping them into an email thread. Ask them to keep a digital or handwritten journal of their experiences. You can then sit down with the new performer and discuss what they have experienced, and, specifically, what steps they will take on the next service call.

What if the learner needs to be stronger at leading team meetings? This is an easy one. After taking a short course on better meeting management (more on this in the next section), sit down with the learner and help them plan an upcoming meeting. Provide support and encouragement for the spaces where the learner feels unsure. And, of course, guide that learner to feel even more successful in advance of next week's challenge.

Follow-up, follow-up, follow-up

Follow-up takes place at three distinct junctures in the learning process (like zone defense!): before, during, and after the learning event.

- **Follow-up before.** Once you know that a learner has signed up for the virtual class, reach out to them to dig further. What are the learner's expectations? Why was this course selected in the first place? What do you both want to be able to DO as a result of the learning experience? When does the learner plan to undertake this self-study experience and what will they do as a result? Share your ideas and ask the learner to share their ideas. This will create buy-in and encourage the learner. They'll know that you are tuned into their success.
- **Follow-up during.** This happens immediately after the learner has participated in the training. Ask the learner how it went verbally or with a short survey. What did they learn? What are their first and immediate take-aways? Was this time well spent? How can you help the learner apply the learning? Now that they have participated in the course, they may have some new ideas and insights into doing things differently.
- **Follow-up after.** Lastly, this happens as you work with the learner to implement the learning. Provide support without removing the responsibility to do the job on their own. Assist by removing obstacles and

providing all the necessary resources the learner will need. Encourage the learner as they try new things that may be outside of their current comfort zone.

When you take these steps, you'll assure a better learning experience regardless of whether or not the learning takes place in the classroom or through a screen.

Virtual classrooms are a wonderful way to deliver training. These simple guidelines add a page in your playbook for your team of learners to succeed.

BETTER MEETINGS, STRONGER TEAMS

While the way we get work done has undoubtedly evolved, the business environment is just as demanding, competitive, and perhaps even more complicated than ever before. It's up to leaders to make meetings an essential tool for high performance teams.

Reaching your targets is impacted not only by individual performers, but also by the team and how well these individuals work together. We all know the drain on productivity caused by personality conflicts, miscommunication, and conflicting priorities. And nowhere do these team vulnerabilities present themselves more vividly than in team meetings.

As critical as they are to help you move the ball forward, meetings can be fraught with wrong turns and roadblocks that are easily prevented with just a little bit of pre-planning.

Below is a list of suggestions to boost your team's performance during meetings. While hardly all-inclusive, this list applies to any kind of team meeting you lead, be it a specific project team or a group of direct reports. The goal is to avoid the Wild Wild West free-for-all that ensues from lack of structure and accountability. Each suggestion will hinge on what your team members say and do before, during, and after the meeting, and it's up to you to hold them accountable.

Here are a few tips: plan for extra room space based on the number of attendees; provide socially distanced seating and proper personal protective equipment (PPE); and create individual "kits" with pens, markers, and other meeting tools so people don't have to share.

While there may be a few new rules to meetings, the old tried and true standards still bear repeating:

- On the front end, establish a set of ground rules around interruptions, methods of consensus, and following up on shared agreements.
- Provide an agenda ahead of time so that everyone on the team can weigh in.
- When in the actual meeting, open by stating the meeting purpose clearly, even if you assume that everyone knows why they are attending.
- Assign a meeting note taker and agree on the execution of next steps.
- Start on time, involve everyone with open-ended questions, and wrap up by agreeing on who will do what by when before the next meeting.

If a meeting takes place virtually, here are some additional tips:

- Take attendance with a verbal check-in or a raised hand at the beginning of the meeting or at the break.
- Record the meeting so those unable to attend can review at another time (big advantage to keep people in the loop). Ask people to share their thoughts and ideas. This is always important to do, even when face-to-face, but you'll need to do this *more frequently* in a virtual setting.
- Pause longer than usual to allow people to gather their thoughts, come off mute, and respond.
- You may have to call individuals out by name–although this is not a first choice–if you are struggling to get participation, which is typically lower in virtual settings.
- You may want to plant a few "ready" participants who know they may be called on and so won't be caught off guard.

If the meeting extends past a break, and this holds true for both face-to-face and virtual meetings, ask someone to summarize before moving forward to remind everyone of the progress you've made and pick up any loose ends.

Improvements don't end here. What you do after the meeting can make a big difference in the team's actions.

- Issue a link to the recording.
- Send out slides or other visuals if the meeting included these.
- Ask for additional input after the meeting on a team chat site or intranet.

- Make sure everyone updates this location as they make progress on their action items.
- Ask employees to rate their satisfaction with the meeting on a simple five-point scale using five as "very satisfied" and one if the group interactions need "significant improvement."

You can gather this data via email to maintain a touch-free poll and then employ new ways to improve your next meeting.

Meetings are just one of the many processes that have no doubt changed in your workplace. Keep in mind these simple yet effective ideas for better meetings and high-performance teams.

THE BIG PLAY: DIVERSITY AND INCLUSION

Diversity and Inclusion, a Conversation with Katherine Ramsey, Vice President Global Human Resources, and Kris Cuthbertson, Training and Operations Special Projects Manager, for G&W Electric

If you walk into one of G&W Electric's plants, you will see immediately a diverse set of employees. You may hear snippets of different languages, see people of all different origins and backgrounds working together, and you will even see flags from all over the world represented on their walls.

Katherine Ramsey, Vice President Global Human Resources, and Kris Cuthbertson, Training and Operations Special Projects Manager, discussed with IMEC how diversity and inclusion developed and thrives at G&W Electric, a global organization of engineers and manufacturing personnel dedicated to finding solutions for the utility, commercial, and industrial sectors. G&W Electric has sales and manufacturing plants worldwide and has remained globally competitive, both in the production and its hiring.

That's not to say that G&W Electric has never run into a problem with racism or discriminatory bullying in its workforce. G&W Electric is a manufacturing company with 1,300 employees worldwide where a variety of personalities come together. The company uses a variety of tools and assessments to talk to employees about what type of communicator they are, how they communicate, how others in the organization communicate, and how to collaborate with their colleagues.

G&W Electric has also run into hiring problems, just like most other manufacturers. In order to expand their already diverse hiring pool and fill their open positions, G&W Electric opened their doors to include a neurodiverse workforce, on top of the dozens of other ways G&W Electric has been an inclusive work environment in the past.

PART ONE: A NEW INITIATIVE FOR DIVERSITY, EQUITY, AND INCLUSION

IMEC: To widen your hiring pool and fill more positions, IMEC had the privilege of working with you and partnering with Autism Workforce, an Illinois-based company dedicated to finding good jobs for capable employees on the Autism spectrum. How did the process start?

KC: We did a tour with our representative from Autism Workforce, teamed him up with our Talent Acquisition Recruiter, and started initial discussions. This included a couple of site visits for Autism Workforce to see what jobs we had available. They wanted to see some work instructions and actually see the job being done.

IMEC: What happened when you got to the interview stage?

KC: [Autism Workforce] reviewed their existing talent pool and said, "We think this group of people will be a good fit. Before the interview, however, we would like to tour the facility with them."

Jack, who is now employed with us, came in with his advisor [through Autism Workforce] and they toured together so they could both witness the job. After that, the candidates went through very brief interviews.

KR: One of the things that I think demonstrated our commitment to making this program work for us is the partnership with Autism Workforce. We took their guidance and actually trained our interviewers on how to interact differently with a candidate who might be neurodiverse. We did some very specific training, which, actually, we learned a lot from.

KC: We got rid of our star philosophy, or our behavior -based interviewing, and asked more pointed questions.

KR: We generally do behavioral based interview training and some knowledge that we took away from our Autism Workforce training was that it's not the right method to elicit the kind of information we would want from someone who's neurodiverse.

KC: The other thing that we did differently was that Autism Workforce actually helped us prepare interview packets so that the candidates would know exactly what they were walking into.

KR: A very personal, comforting approach so that the individuals came in able to be their best selves and present themselves to us in a way so we could understand what they could offer the company.

KC: Part of the interview process was the candidates actually doing the job. We have a lot of jobs that are very simple in nature and very repetitive, but require a lot of attention to detail. During the interview process, they had actually seen the job training aids, videos, and pictures ahead of time, so they were able to come in and prove they could do the job onsite.

IMEC: It sounds like there was a lot of upfront work involved. What made you believe this could be useful to your organization?

KR: Part of what we were doing was 1) trying to widen the hiring pool of individuals we could hire because of the general labor shortage for technical skills and talent that you've probably already written a whole other book on, and 2) as Kris said, we have jobs that are very narrow, but critically important to the product we build. These aren't jobs that we don't care about. These are jobs where certain personality types might be more drawn to and perform better. Our first Autism Workforce recruit, Mario, actually outperformed others in the same role.

KC: By the end of his first shift, he was outperforming our assemblers who do this on a day-to-day basis.

KR: After about two or three days, he was done with his entire weeks' worth of work and asking for more. So, we had an immediate win!

IMEC: You mentioned when we talked to you earlier that you were doing a second round of hiring through Autism Workforce?

KR: Yes, starting next week?

KC: That's right, it is starting next week! We've actually been working with Autism Workforce to develop more videos, more job breakdowns for training aids, and setting up cells in a very color-coded fashion. Today, right now in fact, is our Autism 101 Workforce, which our supervisors, team leads, and people who are going to be working side-by-side with these candidates go through. It's a class teaching them behaviors and other things that might trigger somebody in a neurodiverse workforce.

KR: Our partnership with Autism Workforce teaches us how to approach different people successfully which helps us in many leadership situations. It's another tool in our toolkit, right?

IMEC: I know G&W Electric was already a very diverse workforce, and we will get to that more later, but did adding a neurodiverse workforce create any tension or disruption?

KR: It was a home run. Integrating neurodiverse employees was an adjustment for G&W Electric in some ways, but not the adjustment that I expected. We had employees come forward and talk about what a great place this is to work because they had a child, a sister or brother, a son that had neurodiverse issues.

G&W Electric's employee engagement went up noticeably, and when it was time to find mentors for the new neurodiverse workforce, several employees stepped up and volunteered.

IMEC: How many neurodiverse employees do you think you will have in your company at the end of this year?

KR: As many as we can get.

KC: We'll have at least two that will start immediately.

KR: By year-end, we would like to have as many as 10 or 12. We started with a pilot program, which included 4 employees, one who works in the office.

KC: He's actually taking the American Society for Quality recognized certified calibration technician exam next month.

KR: So that's a promotional opportunity down the road for him. We want to be a place where everyone can contribute, irrespective of their race, gender, sexual orientation, religion, etc. It doesn't matter to us. We want you to be able to come here and positively influence our business. But it starts with understanding that everybody brings a story to work.

PART TWO: HOW DIVERSITY AND INCLUSION CONTRIBUTES TO G&W ELECTRIC

Katherine Ramsey sat back down with IMEC a second time to discuss how diversity and inclusion as a whole has a place at G&W Electric.

IMEC: Overall, G&W Electric's diverse makeup is a natural product of the company's environment. So how did this diversity come about, when so many other manufacturers are struggling to make their workplaces more diverse?

KR: Diversity is not about a quota system. We don't have hiring quotas. Diversity is really about the fact that we're a global company.. We need to have an appreciation of how to think, act, speak, sell, be respectful to all kinds of individuals–customers, suppliers, and vendors across the world. All of that starts with how we treat our employees. Our owner, John Mueller, will say, "Treat the customer right, treat the employee right, and you can't go wrong," and that is exactly our guiding principle.

IMEC: What does G&W Electric care about when hiring employees?

KR: What we care about is the way that an employee performs. Are they creative? Are they innovative? Are they courageous? Are they good risk takers? Do they collaborate well? Do they communicate properly? Can they lead themselves, lead the business, and then lead their teams? Those are the kinds of individuals that we search for.

IMEC: As a global company, do you feel having cultures that represent your customers is essential to staying competitive?

KR: G&W Electric's employees need to have an understanding and appreciation for the cultural background of customers. Insight into how customers think is important, and that comes from people who are not all the same.

Most importantly, diversity is crucial in problem-solving. G&W Electric serves customers through solving their problems, and you need people with different backgrounds and perspectives for a good problem-solving team.

IMEC: For more technically challenging issues, we've seen that you put together 8-step problem-solving teams. Is diversity important to those teams?

KR: [We say] we need this type of thinking, we need this type of skill. When all those thinking styles and skills are put in a group, the result is a creative and diverse team of employees ready to solve customer problems.

IMEC: How does G&W Electric continue to grow as a diverse organization?

KR: We have a very, very active referral program, and it's actually how we hire [the majority] of our manufacturing and production employees. Generally, people refer people like them, and since we're diverse, we keep growing that diverse base.

IMEC: How did G&W Electric become so diverse in the first place?

KR: I think it's because we hire the best. We hire the best people we can find and those people come from all over the world.

IMEC: Even in your U.S. factory, do employees come from all over the world?

KR: Yes, we have a very large Lithuanian base, Eastern European base, Jamaican, Mexican, etc.

What we do is a very niche engineering, and that it is not generally taught in the U.S. and has a very small applicant base. So those individuals are located all over the world. That's not something that is generally taught in the U.S., Sso in order to continue to grow our business, we will have to find those individuals anywhere in the world.

Another aspect about diversity and quotas . . . if someone is trying to manage diversity by a quota or a number system, that's one way. At least it's a way to get started, but for us, it's not the number, it's also what role that person has in the organization – is the role one with influence and decision-making authority? Can they make a difference?

IMEC: What about diversity among your leadership team?

KR: We have nine people on our executive team. We have two women, someone from China, someone from Canada, and someone that's African American. More than half the team is diverse.

Think about how diversity can contribute to your organization. You don't just want twelve people with the same experiences, opinions, mindset, etc., you want twelve people from all variety of all backgrounds in positions that influence your business.

Positions of influence are where you want the most diverse thinking in your organization.

IMEC: How do people from different cultures learn to work together? For example, do you provide cultural awareness training, seminars, and other types of formal initiatives?

KR: Actually, no. We have a philosophy. You build relationships by working together, and we have real jobs for real people with real problems to solve . . . we say here's your job, here's the team that you work with, let's go. We do support them when needed.

IMEC: How does diversity help G&W Electric be globally competitive?

KR: Not all of us are the same. We sell all around the world, and we need more diverse employees to help cater to those customers.

I try very hard, from a value perspective, not to get diversity down to a number. You can have lots of diversity, but if those diverse individuals have no say or influence in your company, who cares if you're diverse.

IMEC: What are some common misconceptions about hiring for diversity?

KR: It does not have to be expensive or difficult because it's not about setting a quota. It's about looking wider. Just look wider. It could be that easy.

IMEC: What advice would you give to another manufacturer who wants to integrate diversity more in their workforce?

1. *You have to want it.*
2. *You have to invest in it.*
3. *You have to invite all employees to speak up and participate.*
4. *You have to widen your hiring pool.*

FILE UNDER DIVERSITY AND INCLUSION

G&W Electric strives to make every employee, no matter their background, feel at home. If an employee has served in an Armed Services branch in any country, that flag is put on their wall. When employees look up and see a flag they were proud to represent, they feel like they belong. This may seem like a small gesture, but it's just another way G&W Electric goes above and beyond to make sure all cultures are represented.

Chapter 3

THE VALUE OF CUSTOMER RELATIONSHIPS

Relentlessly pursue your customer's success.

Time to walk the line.

Our companies are challenged to perform. As leaders, it is easy to take our eye off the fundamentals while dealing with day-to-day business demands and economic uncertainty.

Now it is time to revisit the basics and to reexamine how well you are taking care of your customers. It is time to look at how your key processes are performing. It is time to walk the line, as Johnny Cash croons in his earthy ballad by a similar name.

In this chapter, you will get a refresher on building customer relationships and what it takes to understand them better through the elusive but always essential voice of customer. We'll also take a look at what it means to build your reputation through your brand and how to identify your ideal customer.

One recurring topic among manufacturers is the customer experience. We'll unpack that, too, from your prospects finding you through Search Engine Optimization (SEO) to marketing outreach to building customer rapport. Lastly, we'll close the chapter talking about gaining client commitments to move opportunities forward and chat with Chris Blumhoff, Chief Operating Officer at F.N. Smith Corporation, on his big play views around sales and marketing (prepare for some game-changing insights).

INNOVATING YOUR CUSTOMER SERVICE

There's always someone in the crowd who looks at a Jackson Pollock painting and says, "I could splatter paint on a canvas and make one of those." So often, the easiest looking things can be the hardest to do well (like making paint splatters evoke emotion–and sell for $140 million as Pollock's "No. 5, 1948" painting did in 2006). Listening to customers might be in that category as it is also easily taken for granted.

Why is this? Customers will not always say what they feel or, simply, your customer's needs have evolved over time. If you've listened well throughout the relationship, you'll likely not be caught unaware.

Nurturing Customer Relationships

Listening starts with regularly scheduled virtual or in-person meetings with key customers. (A commonly accepted statistic is that a new customer is five times more expensive to obtain than expanding your footprint with an existing customer.) Questions to ask include the following:

- How have you been doing? Personally? As a company?
- How does business look over the next few months? The next year?
- How has your chief problem changed in the past year?
- What challenges do you see in the next three months for your company?
- What new challenges are you experiencing that you haven't faced before?
- What does success look like?
- How are you executing against the above points?

Make no assumptions. Just have a deep conversation. Take good notes. If possible, talk not only to your customer's key contact but also their frontline employees who receive your product.

Understanding Customer Touch Points

With these insights in hand, talk with your team in reverse order of how your products are made so that you clearly see through the lens of your customer. Start with the employees who have the last points of customer contact. For example, this might be product delivery/warehouse, customer service, and invoicing. Ask similar questions like these:

- How are you and your family doing?
- How do you think we are doing as a company?
- What are you concerned about in the upcoming months? Excited about?
- What problems do we need to solve?
- What "above and beyond" actions are we doing or do you recommend we do to improve the customer experience?

Work backwards. Who in the company is involved in the process step before these final points of contact? Visit the production line and office support roles. Have the same conversation. Then the next process step. And keep going until you have walked to the first point of customer contact. Perhaps it is the sales team or even your webmaster who receives inquiries through your website.

For each interaction, listen intently and take good notes. Follow-up with any urgent concerns or questions that are not easily answered during the discussions.

You now have a long list of insights you can use to strengthen your customer service. You will learn about gaps in performance, and perhaps walk away with new and innovative ways to serve at higher levels. Embrace the knowledge you gain to help your company find new innovations in service.

Competing at a Higher Level

High performance competitors accept critical feedback–and then act on it. Share your newly found insight with your leadership team, product team, customer service, R&D, and marketing. Informing everyone gives them fresh perspective into the customer experience so they can better support your mission. If you've gleaned customer testimonials or have the start of a success story, follow-through to write those up and ask for customer approval from those you interviewed.

Your customer's perception of your company is your brand so if you are listening between the lines, you will know what they really think. In fact, the American Marketing Association's list of marketing definitions cites that the International Organization for Standardization (ISO) brand standards define brand as "an intangible asset" that is intended to create "distinctive images and associations in the minds of stakeholders, thereby generating economic benefit/values."[23]

As you listen to your customers closely, you'll be able to see more clearly what sets your brand apart in the minds of your customers. This is your reputation, and it is one of the most important business assets you have. In fact, according to brand marketing firm Losasso, 70% of B2B respondents cite company reputation as the most influential factor when choosing a company to do business with.[24]

Lastly, and perhaps most importantly, identify three to five customer service action items to improve upon. Here, "customer" can refer to both external and internal (department to department). This cannot be an exercise only done on paper, but rather action that produces a noticeable change for the better. Your employees and customers will appreciate it. They will remember how you were the one who took the time to listen.

CUSTOMER JOURNEY MAPS: CREATING AN EXTRAORDINARY CUSTOMER EXPERIENCE

Journey maps are very popular tools, and with good reason. They are a simple, fast, and effective way to help a team understand the experiences that customers are having with an organization from the customers' point of view.

However, like many "simple" things, doing a mapping exercise can be quite a bit more complicated than it first appears. Journey maps are actually a category of different tools, not a single exercise.

Once you get on board with the basic idea—*"Let's map our customer experience to understand the current state and design a better one"*—there can be a bewildering amount of vagueness about what to do next.

There are some beautiful examples of map artifacts online, but how do teams get there? And with journey maps approaching "trendy" status, the state of practice is all over the board, with a lot of bad or half-baked efforts adding noise alongside the work of skilled practitioners.

If you're willing to dig into a good book (another book, we mean), read Jim Kalbach's Mapping Experiences: A Complete Guide to Creating Value through Journeys, Blueprints, and Diagrams. In it, Kalbach writes, "Empathy is about seeing the world through someone else's eyes. It's about an implicit sense of what an experience is like, what people value, and what emotions are involved." Well said.

Here is an outline of the customer journey mapping process.

Before You Begin: Pick Your Team

The right mapping team size is six to eight people: two researchers who will be doing the interviews and facilitating the mapping, plus key participants from across your organization. If there are less than six people, you probably don't have a broad enough interest to justify the activity, and if there are more than eight in the group, dynamics start to get bogged down.

If you don't have an executive director or COO or some other leader keenly interested in understanding and improving the journey you're mapping, you should question if you're actually ready to go. The following shows what a customer mapping exercise might look like.

DAY 1: CHARTING THE COURSE

Start with a half-day or full-day session with the mapping team focused on getting everyone pointed in the same direction. There are four key activities for this session.

1. State your design goal or challenge. Clearly answer the question: "What is driving our organization to do this?" For example:

- For Make-A-Wish Illinois: *How might we create Wish Journeys that produce resiliency in children and their families?*
- For a children's hospital: *How might we create holistic ER visit journeys that provide appropriate physical and emotional care for children and parents?*

- For a financial services firm: *How might we assist younger consumers in their early experiences with money?*

Some of these design challenges are more exploratory and some are very specific. The journeys listed above represent:

- An end-to-end customer journey with Make-A-Wish.
- A journey through one specific part of the children's hospital's services.
- A whole "season of life" experience beyond the boundaries of interaction with the financial services firm.

2. Pick the map's point of view. What is the starting point, ending point, and boundaries of the journey you are mapping? The better you can articulate whose experience you are mapping and when that experience begins and ends, the more impactful your mapping exercise will be. Spend time getting this nailed down.

3. Create a persona or personas of the people who will be in your map. Some maps have only one persona or audience description, which is totally fine (and usually preferred). A good rule of thumb is seven to ten interviews per persona in the map, so adding personas will increase the interview and mapping effort in a directly linear way. If this is your first map, I'd recommend forcing yourself to narrow down to a single persona with a tightly defined beginning and end.

A word of warning: It is tempting to not pick a tightly defined persona here because you want to cast your net widely to learn as much as possible. However, if the people you interview (and, thus, the journey you map) are not fairly similar, you could find meaningful divergence in experiences when you are mapping. This makes the map—which is already somewhat complex with granular experience data—feel completely overwhelming, even to the point of being meaningless, as the team can no longer grasp and order the patterns in the map.

It is relatively easy to pick another persona, do seven to ten more interviews, and lay that over the existing map to look for differences. On the other hand, it is really hard to make an initial map without a tightly defined persona and point of view.

4. Hypothesize which stages are on the journey. Make an "inside out" guess at the stages of the journey you are preparing to map.

Your team should include team members who know the journey you are mapping really well from the organization's point of view. So, get some big stickies and create a list of the "stages" of the journey as they understand it. Give each stage a name, stick them on the wall from start to finish, and get an agreement in the room that these stages accurately describe the journey. These are not your final journey map stages (those will come from your interviews), but they help everyone get oriented to what you think is true of the journey at a high level.

Phew, day one in the books. It goes faster after this.

WEEK ONE: PREPARING TO INTERVIEW

The rest of week one you'll be doing three things:

1. Create a field guide. A field guide is, in its simplest form, a list of interview questions. These are questions your team believes can help participants narrate their experiences that are of particular interest to the journey you are mapping.

As you prepare, remember you are looking to uncover experiences, not opinions. This means your first question should be something like:

"Tell me about the first time you ever heard of [our organization]."

or

"Tell me when you first realized you needed [the thing] that [our organization] provides."

Every question after that should be for the purpose of helping the person remember and recount their experience. Try to get them to narrate a documentary about their experience. Then dig in to look for the specific emotions, thoughts, and actions along the way, with particular attention to places where it seems like something is not going well.

Do not ask for their opinion or advice about how things went or what you could have done better. Stay laser focused on their retelling of the actual experience as it was.

2. Schedule interviews. Pick interviewees who match your persona and who are trustworthy. Schedule about thirty-minute interviews with them and, while having prepared questions is essential, keep the interview unstructured so it becomes an enlightening two-way conversation.

If you're not using existing customers for the map you picked, you may want to use a sourcing agency. If you're doing it yourself, use something like a scheduling app similar to Calendly to make scheduling a bit easier. You'll typically need forty-five to sixty minutes for an interview, and you'll want to provide a thank you gift of some kind to your participants. Gift cards are de jour, but more specific or thoughtful gifts are always good.

Sourcing and scheduling always takes more time than teams anticipate, so even though four days seems like plenty of time to get interview prep done, you'll need to focus here to get your interviews in place.

3. Make a data packet. Identify any other data your organization already has that may be relevant to the map. Many organizations have survey feedback data (quantitative and qualitative), usage/repeat buyer data, and other information that can be valuable in supplementing the interviews for the map. Use the time when you aren't sourcing and scheduling to identify this information, curate it, and prepare a "packet" to be distributed to the team before mapping.

WEEK TWO: INTERVIEWS AND CODING

We typically leave a week of elapsed time for interviews. Some tips for successful interviewing are the following:

- Stick to two to three interviews per day.
- Interview in pairs, with one person asking the questions and the other taking notes.
- Ask for permission to record the interview and do so.
- Immediately after the interview, both interviewers should work together to code the interview into the thoughts, feelings, actions, etc. that compose a journey map.

At the end of week two, distribute all of the data you have collected to the full mapping team. This means the data packet curated in week one, the coded interviews created in week two, and—optional for those who are interested—the recorded interviews themselves. Ask your team to spend at least half a day reading through all of the interviews and data before you meet to map. Everyone *must* be familiar with the data before the mapping session.

I hate to even admit this, but I once let a client convince us to lead them through a journey map without doing interviews, just to let their team see the exercise. The end result is that their team accurately saw journey mapping as pointless, which is exactly what it is without interviews. So, don't be dumb like me: never skip interviews.

WEEK THREE: MAP!

The first three days of this week are simply for the team to have time to read and absorb all the data, and for you to collect all of the color-coded sticky notes you need to fill a wall with the incredible map you are about to produce. The last two days are for making the map and responding to it.

1. Make the map. Mapping is actually really simple if you've done all of the prep work well. Plan for six hours together, with a healthy break for lunch. Normal, good facilitation skills apply here:

- No devices in the room
- Regular breaks
- Good snacks/low carbs
- Get people out of their seats to keep the energy up

Start by naming the first stage in the shared journeys narrated across the interviews. Use a really big sticky and put it up high on the wall. Then, underneath it, fill in that stage with *Actions* first, then *Thoughts* and *Feelings*, then finally *Touchpoints* and *Channels.* We call these the customer experience (CX) Building Blocks, and define them using the questions below:

THOUGHTS	How are people framing or evaluating their experience? What do they expect?
FEELINGS	What emotions do people have along the way? What are the highs? What are the lows?
ACTIONS	What effort are people expending?
TOUCHPOINTS	Person with need - Organization with stuff
CHANNELS	The medium through which the Touchpoint is conveyed.
OPPORTUNITIES	Digital Transformation - Process Improvement -Training - Research - Process Improvement -

Typically, we print out a poster-sized version of the image above and put it up in the room while we're journey mapping.

Each Building Block should have a specific color of sticky, which will run in a horizontal row across the wall through each stage. Then, repeat with the second stage. This process isn't fully linear, and you'll find yourself skipping ahead and doubling back a bit as the map emerges and insights come out.

As a facilitator, you'll need to get a feel for when enough is enough in each stage. Some stages are naturally more dense than others, so don't feel pressure to make them all look equal. And have the courage to say "no" to a suggested sticky if it is duplicative or not clearly indicated in the interviews. You'll end up with a lot on the wall regardless.

2. Identify opportunities. This requires three to six hours together, on the very next day after you make the map.

You are going to "mine" the map for opportunities. It is important to keep this on a separate day, both to get new energy into the room and to be sure the mapping day doesn't veer too quickly into trying to come up with solutions.

Mining for opportunities works best as an "alone together" exercise, where the team gets fifteen minutes to peruse the map silently, each person making notes to themselves, and another fifteen minutes to write down the clearest opportunities they see in the journey.

Then the team takes turns, each person going up to the map to present their stickies, briefly explain each opportunity, and stick it on the wall in the appropriate stage. Similar and identical opportunities can be grouped together for clarity.

After this, go through some form of ranking exercise for

the opportunities. We like to use a simple feasibility and impact scale, so the lowest effort and highest reward opportunities float to the top, but any sort of ranking activity will work. If there are lots of opportunities, it can help to use a straw poll (each member gets approximately eight little stickers to put on the opportunities they want to vote for) in order to narrow down to a workable number for ranking.

Finally, pick the top three to four opportunities and create a simple plan for each one on what you might do to learn and execute against that opportunity to improve or transform the journey. Each team approaches this step differently, and whatever is typical for your organization can work.

The Map Artifact

Now, at the very end, it is time to consider a map artifact.

First, know that the activity of mapping is the purpose of mapping, not the artifact. You can have a totally successful mapping activity and never produce an artifact. The role of the artifact is to communicate your insights to other people in the organization. If you need to do that, make a map. If you don't, then don't.

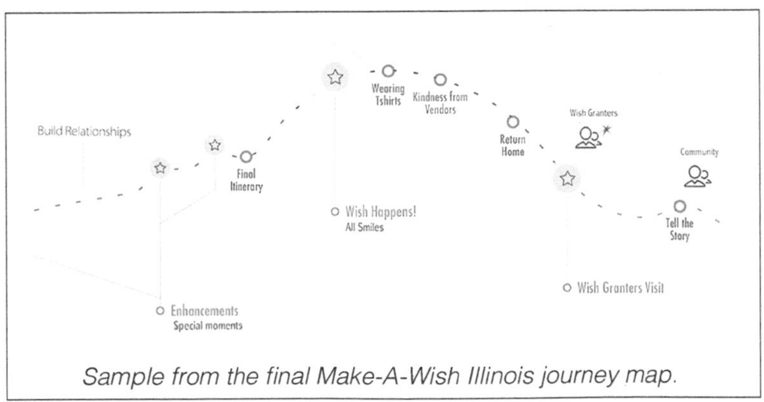

Sample from the final Make-A-Wish Illinois journey map.

There are map templates floating around the internet, but the best maps use a bespoke design to really communicate what is happening in the experience.

And that's it! Three weeks to your first map. Now you can repeat with a different point of view or persona, and execute on the insights and opportunities this map generated. Happy mapping.

IMEC wishes to thank Jon Berbaum, President of Highland Solutions, for contributing to Made in Illinois.

CATEGORIZING CUSTOMERS

In Richard Koch's 1998 book, *The 80/20 Principle*, he refers to the tipping point as an invisible line separating the 80% from the 20%. He implies that a great deal of effort (the 80%) can be put into a new product, a program, or a new social platform, without making significant progress. Many give up before reaching the tipping point. Those that persist and push through to the tipping point reap the benefits of huge success. This reflects on the core concept of 80/20, in that 80% of your business results come from 20% of your activity. Inversely, 80% of your activity only influences 20% of your results.

Here is the great news behind 80/20: the method identifies significant waste in the value stream and provides clear opportunities to remove the waste, and make tremendous leaps forward in productivity, value, and customer engagement.

Reassess and Solidify Relationships with Your Top Customers

As of the time of this writing, we continue to "work through" the pandemic. As your customers emerge from the crisis, you will notice something interesting. Some may have been thriving during this time, while others may have been merely surviving. Are your top customers pre-crisis still the top customers post-crisis?

'A' customers generate the lion's share of revenue and profits. Focus on this group. To identify top customers, list customers by annual sales, sorted by highest to lowest. Next, divide the total number of customers by four. The top fourth are 'A' customers, and the next fourth are 'B' customers, the next group are 'C's, and the final are 'D' customers.

Make certain prior annual sales are still generally in line with your forecasts. Be aware markets may significantly change during rebound, and customers previously perceived as a low value 'D' may suddenly become a higher value, while an 'A' customer may have dropped lower, or even be knocked out of the market.

Realign Strategy for Future Success

Once the reassessment of top customers is complete, realigning strategy is of paramount importance. Alter your strategy to better serve the core 'A' customers, as well as moving away from low value customers and products. It helps the company to focus on primary markets and rebound with the strongest value proposition and a competitive advantage. A simple tool broadly applied to set priority is a high-low grid that uses "Easy to Do/Hard to Do" on one axis and "High Impact/Low Impact" on the other. The highest priority strategies would be "Easy to Do/High Impact" and the ones that should be shelved would be "Hard to Do/Low Impact".

Once the strategic plan and supporting sales and operations plan have been reassessed for the rebound, it is critical to implement or update the business operating system to ensure execution of the plan. Business operating systems help establish goals, timelines, and accountability. A typical system will include daily, weekly, monthly, and quarterly progress reviews. Examples include the following:

- Daily: Safety, quality, delivery, and productivity
- Weekly: Cash flow and inventory levels
- Monthly: Change in cash, A/R aging, comparisons, and analysis ratios
- Quarterly: Risk management, 80/20 analysis (update), supply chain costs, and pricing strategy review

Use the business operating system as a day-to-day playbook and a litmus test to evaluate new projects or activity. If it doesn't fit within the system, it likely doesn't align with the strategy.

Focus on Employees

The most important part of any strategy, and certainly the most critical 20% of a business's assets, is the workforce that makes it all possible. Look after the team, from the shop to the top. Provide clear and open communication and let everyone know there is a shifting strategy in play. Visually share metrics, including progress and setbacks and create a feedback loop from the front line. Keep an open mind for improvements and gather suggestions. Use 80/20 principles to assess incoming ideas and select those with the highest payback that are easiest to implement. Reserve other ideas for continuous improvement.

Working on the Business Improves Performance

Much of the advice outlined above is just good business practice but can be easy to set aside when facing daily challenges. Focus on what is most important during this time. One of Koch's observations was: "I have observed thousands of examples of the 80/20 Principle, I have had my faith reinforced: faith in progress, in great leaps forward, and in mankind's ability, individually and collectively, to improve the hand that nature has dealt."

BUILDING RAPPORT IS A STEP TOWARD UNDERSTANDING THE VOICE OF YOUR CUSTOMER

Jay Conrad Levinson shot to fame as the author of the marketing classic *Guerrilla Marketing.* The late author wrote: "In order to sell a product or a service, a company must establish a relationship with the consumer. It must build trust and rapport. It must understand the customer's needs, and it must provide a product that delivers the promised benefits."

Merriam-Webster defines rapport as: "a relationship

characterized by agreement, mutual understanding, or empathy that makes communication possible or easy."

When it comes to building rapport, keep it simple and listen, listen, listen! It is all about trust and relationships. People do not do business with companies; people do business with people.

Before you go to a company's facility or pitch a new account virtually, do your homework: know your customer and their products, find a mutual subject and focus on it at the start of the conversation, know the background of the person you are speaking with by studying their LinkedIn profile, and research the decision influencers for your product at your prospect's facility.

Be aware of your prospect's world, starting with the town the company is located in (even if your favorite sports team is an archrival, it goes a long way to mention something about another person's hometown favorite). Find common ground based on your knowledge of the prospect. Did they go to a university you have visited? Do they post about green initiatives? Are they a Chicago Bears fan on Facebook? Be responsible and listen, listen, listen; when it is your turn to talk, mention a subject you heard them talk about. Keep this conversation going as long as they are comfortable with it. Keep the subject about them and their company. People like to talk about themselves and hear less about you–reply in reference to them. Keep the conversation positive. If they mention a negative, transform it into a positive.

Going an extra mile to walk in another's shoes is the heart of understanding others and building rapport.

Present your services as an opportunity and investment rather than a cost. People like to think they are getting a good deal to rationalize the investment. Mention similar projects that you have had success with in the past and identify positive values from actual projects.

On average, it takes seven to eleven touch points to convert a customer. Ask prospects if you can add them to your newsletter subscription list so you are consistently in front of them (more on inside lists in the next section), if only to have them see your brand pop up in the subject line of their email inbox. If your company has a blog, send it to your prospect the day it is published as a way to educate and stay in touch.

Over time, you will learn about your customer's needs. Continue the conversation around them and note several subjects to follow up with using specific data to support their request. Establish a return response, call/email, or additional site visits to share your specific findings that can assist them.

The more you learn about your customers, the more information you have to identify the voice of the customer (VOC). Go back to the customer journey mapping exercise mentioned earlier in this chapter and note major customer touchpoints. Your customers interact with you on many levels: sales, operations, R&D, customer service, invoicing and accounting, shipping and receiving, at the receptionist's desk, every time they call. How will you capture what they are thinking and feeling? VOC programs can be as simple as an annual survey, post-delivery survey, focus groups, or regular one-on-one debriefs. *Quality Magazine* explains two types of VOC data for manufacturers: reactive and proactive. Reactive data includes "complaints, compliments, feedback, hotline data, product returns, and/or warranty claims." Proactive data "can be collected from customer interviews, surveys, focus groups, observations, and/or test customers."[25] Building rapport considers all of these as well as the two-way art of listening to others.

Levinson helps us draw a straight line to the value of building trust and rapport by understanding the voice of the customer. What you learn will help your manufacturing company to take action to improve, creating more momentum as a global competitor willing to listen, support, and invest in its customers.

CREATING SALES OPPORTUNITIES IN A VIRTUAL WORLD

In 2018, CSO Insights, the research arm of Miller Heiman Group, found that more than 70% of B2B (business-to-business) buyers fully define their needs before engaging with a sales representative. For Illinois manufacturers, this fact means that employing virtual sales strategies will help prospects find you more easily on the web, produce more warm leads (prospects who are more familiar with your company) while moving them along the sales journey faster (from awareness to becoming a customer!).

Sales in a virtual world could be a book all on its own (and it probably already is ten times over). In the manufacturing sector, we're taking a look at three tools deserving of your time and attention: Search Engine Optimization (SEO means your website ranks as high as possible on search engines such as Google or Yahoo! when people type in specific search terms), content strategy, and the better-than-gold inside list. These are simple yet powerful tools to nurture prospect and customer relationships, because winning more business from existing customers accelerates your competitiveness and gives you a good reason to celebrate with your team. Let's take a look at this trio.

What is SEO? SEO is the ongoing work required to:

- Build credibility for your website with search engines.
- Ensure you are connecting with the appropriate seekers for your products/services–with search engine support.
- Leverage your website to be an efficient marketing and lead generation tool (lead generation in this case can take the form of a submitted contact form or someone calling you from your website).
- Attract the best potential customers to your website.

SEO makes you more findable. If you conducted the customer journey mapping exercise outlined earlier in this chapter, then perhaps you discovered your prospects first search for you online (also called the moment of truth, this is where prospects type in the keywords they use in order to search for the solution to their problem). Static websites will sink in search results over time, falling out of favor with search engines. An SEO program allows you to maximize a website's value by bringing qualified and interested traffic to it, which is typically the objective of a website.

SEO requires regular work to be done on the website, as well as beyond it, to get the attention from search engines, and to ultimately rise up in search rankings (the end goal).

The point of SEO is to accurately attract quality visitors to a website, visitors who are seeking specific types of products and services. Essentially, the idea is to strategically focus on the best types of customers, creating content that really *speaks* to them, their everyday pains and frustrations, and helps to provide a solution through your products and services.

Like so many aspects of doing business, technology has changed the face of SEO drastically in a few short years. There was a time when regularly updating your website with a new photo or content would indicate to search engines that your site was active and being maintained. This was a necessary activity to increase in search rankings–back in the day.

Today, there is "on page" and "off page" work that must be completed on a consistent basis in order to maintain your site's reputation and rise in the search rankings. On page work, or the parts of the website visitors can see, ensures your content resonates with customers and is critical in showing search engines that you are worthy of having relevant traffic sent to your website. This is critical in attracting "warm" visitors, and not those who bounce off the homepage, wondering how they landed there in the first place. There are other initial structural checks and balances to be made as well, ensuring the site is in proper form to be indexed by search engines.

Off page work, or the parts of the website visitors cannot see, includes creating content using your specific keywords and keyword phrases solely for the purpose of search engines to source. There are many websites that search engines use to provide an indication as to whether a website is credible. Humans are not the audience for this content, and it is to be created and written to connect with robots and crawlers. Those creative writing skills learned in school will not be exercised on this piece of SEO work. Other off page work to be accomplished includes backlinks, which are links from other websites to yours. This is like a vote of confidence from an objective source–also something search engines value highly in serving up your website to those seeking your products and services. This link tells search engines like Google that your content is so highly trusted, another website is linking to it.

One critical aspect of moving up in the SEO rankings is being knowledgeable of changes in what Google expects of websites. Some larger changes are well publicized, such as mobile responsive design. But there is also continuous tweaking to the algorithm (an algorithm is how a search engine likes Google "crawls" or checks out a website. This algorithm tells their robots to check for certain credentials that ranks the site higher or lower in the search engine).

The algorithm is not publicized, leaving the person at your company (or your digital marketing firm) responsible for doing this work to make continuous adjustments in the SEO program as a result. For example, with the rise of voice search, there is Answer Engine Optimization (AEO). Voice commerce is changing the way people find solutions to problems.

The good news is SEO doesn't have to be overwhelming at all. Technology has provided some great tools for SEO experts who do this work to be more efficient, measurable, and scalable. In fact, SEO has become a very affordable part of a marketing program that can be outsourced to professionals.

What is a content strategy? Content strategy is the content that you publish regularly. This might be on social media, by email to an inside list (we'll talk about that in a moment), success stories available on your website, a blog, e-guides, a podcast, even a book (like the one you are holding!). The strategy behind the content you put out needs to be laser focused.

One place to start is by writing a content mission statement. Like a company mission statement, a content mission statement clearly states your audience, the types of content you will deliver, and the outcome your content will help deliver. For example, the content mission statement for IMEC is: "We create helpful tips and checklists, industry-specific insights, and inspiring stories for Illinois manufacturers so they can move forward faster."

Mapping out a simple content strategy always comes back to your business imperatives. What do you want your company to achieve? Then, connect the types of content you create so it supports your business imperatives. Some companies choose a content theme–like supply chain management, culture, or a future industry trend–and then amplify that theme out each quarter. Others create an editorial calendar that lists the topics they want to expound on.

The best content strategy is rooted in authenticity. Explore topics of interest and relevance to your customers. What questions are they asking? What do they need to know more about to be successful? How can you explore solutions they are seeking?

What is your inside list? Lastly, the inside list is one of your best competitive weapons. These are the contacts who have opted in to receive your information via email. A monthly newsletter or email keeps you top of mind for customers who are not yet ready to buy, but who value you and your content.

MARKETING TO NEW CUSTOMERS WHEN ORDERS ARE SLOW

There is a tendency to cut back on marketing activities in tough or lean times. In fact, the opposite should be the obvious choice. These are exactly the times when your presence can make a difference in growing customers and revenues. No matter the size, there still is a market. The following are ideas to create a short-term plan and approach:

Talk to your customers. Ask about their concerns and pains. There could be a range of issues they are confronted with, from supply chain delays, ability to produce and deliver, or slow or canceled orders from customers. Those same concerns and pains are likely relevant to prospective customers as well and understanding them will serve you well in marketing to both customers and prospects.

Knowing your customer's circumstances allows you to

minimize the effect of those concerns. Use creativity to assist them in filling gaps and solving problems. Is there more work you can do internally, such as assembly? Is it possible to partner with complementary service providers to give more of a total solution? What flexibilities are you able to offer?

Make a list of the customer's needs and how you will address them. The customer pains you understand and solutions you can provide will become part of your marketing messaging. Write down each challenge and how you can address them. Your customers and prospects want to know what is in it for them, particularly in difficult times, so go beyond providing just a list of capabilities.

Get your message out. Having identified customer pains and solutions, begin communicating in channels available to you that will allow your message to get to customers and prospective customers as quickly as possible. Use what you have in place now. There are many options available that are low to no cost. For example, if you only have the means to make phone calls, then make phone calls. You can plan for future, more comprehensive marketing practices later (no need to boil the ocean all in one day!).

Update your website. Your website is the top channel for anyone seeking solutions to problems and should be included in all other forms of your messaging. Update your website copy to reflect new information so that customers and prospects alike can clearly understand how you can support them. Keep their success and minimization of business disruption in mind, using thoughts such as these:

- We are here for you
- We understand your current needs
- We are dependable
- We are flexible
- This is how we can help . . .

Once you have the message created, it is there to be used across other channels listed below.

Phone calls. If this is your only means of engaging with your customers, simply call them to share your message. Multiple people working on this as a team is helpful.

Email. Again, address the known pains and how you support them. A tip here: less is more. Don't write a lengthy email. No one has the time and a lot of words on a page may be ignored. Focus on the facts with an element of genuine caring and empathy. Remember: *We're here for you, dependable, flexible, and this is how we can help. Call us to talk about your unique situation.*

Social media. Platforms like LinkedIn, Twitter, and Facebook are a fast and free connection to your network, and an appropriate way to reach customers and prospects with a supportive message. This is two-way engagement in the moment.

After things settle and going forward. If you don't currently have a communication or marketing program in place, think about building one. Perhaps you have some employees with extra time to work on the necessary tools and plans. Communicating with customers and your market in a nimble fashion will serve you well in good and difficult times. Build relationships to build momentum.

IDENTIFY YOUR BEST CUSTOMERS

Diversify your base of customers, seek out opportunities, and make changes to stay ahead of the competition by more accurately identifying your best customers.

Don't forget your current customers. Your competitors are also marketing to your customers, so stay engaged with them. Many companies are surprised when they lose their top customer even though the signs were there all along. It is easier to generate additional revenue from those loyal to you, rather than building new relationships. Both activities need to co-exist to help you diversify your customer base.

Identify your audiences. Who needs your products and services most? Are there new applications for them? Create a tactical plan for outreach and engagement. This is a strategic exercise in understanding the differences among your targets.

- Think about the person and position title you most want to reach. Typically, this is someone who has influence and decision-making authority in purchasing products and services.

- Identify their pains, frustrations, and challenges–these could differ based on industry segment.
- Identify where each is likely to source information. For example, some positions avoid social media while others are more open to it.
- Identify your capabilities to resolve those pains, frustrations, and challenges.
- Know your competitor's weaknesses with regard to the same pains, frustrations, and challenges.

Identify which channels of communication are best to reach your targets. Depending on the position title of your target, they may choose various channels of communication. Some are more likely to read emails, while others will incorporate LinkedIn or go directly to a Google search and websites.

Understanding as much as you can about your prospective audience will help you strategically create your messaging. Address relevant issues for each segment for a better chance of messages being read, your website being sourced, and your phone call taken. Your messaging should be created as if you were sitting across the table from them. There may be similarities in messaging to each target segment, but if there are differing pains, there should be tailored conversations that resonate and are relevant to each.

A robust SEO program is one of the most important tools for low-cost lead generation. It sets the path for future scalable growth. Leverage your website and use the search engines to attract the most optimum leads. SEO works behind the scenes 24/7 to serve up those interested prospects searching the internet at any given time.

Measure. Knowing what is working and what isn't working will allow you to shift resources to maximize your ROI, in both time and dollars. Tracking incoming call sources, contact forms, email inquiries, Google analytics (available for free when you have a website), and referrals leads to greater efficiency, cost effectiveness, and success in retaining and acquiring new customers.

SHARED COMMITMENTS MOVE SALES OPPORTUNITIES FORWARD

Manufacturing sales teams are required to secure meetings, identify opportunities, and close deals that speak to the long game. This puts even greater emphasis on manufacturing pipelines.

One way to keep opportunities moving through the pipeline is having a mindset of shared commitments between the sales team and prospective clients. Shared commitments are activities or deliverables that must be accomplished in order to ensure the right solution is being proposed, everyone who needs to be involved is, and that the expected outcome is executed on both sides.

Marching through these commitments with a client team using a shared action plan (designed by both sales teams and their clients) is a good way to keep both sides engaged on a shared vision of what "done" looks like. Consider having a shared action plan on a cloud platform so that all parties involved can view and update tasks, status, and details.

Helping prospective clients through the buying process builds relationships and heightens the customer experience on the horizon. Being the resident expert who is able to guide them through the journey might be just what is needed to get to "yes" a little quicker, a little more often, and with deeper, long-term commitment.

THE BIG PLAY: SALES AND MARKETING

A Conversation with Chris Blumhoff, Chief Operating Officer F.N. Smith Corporation in Oregon, IL

Chris Blumhoff was actually a proud IMEC employee before accepting the job of a lifetime. As Chief Operating Officer of F.N. Smith, he oversees the family-owned establishment. When Blumhoff stepped in, what do you think his first task was as COO? Creating a sales department practically from scratch.

Previously, the owner would go out in the field and sell, come back, and then help everybody make what they needed to make. When sales dipped, he would go sell-sell-sell again.

The family knew that this couldn't last forever, so about eight to ten years ago they hired a consultant to help with selling. The consultant told F.N. Smith to give all their engineers commission incentives because they are the ones who talk to customers every day. "We are an engineer-to-order shop and so that bumped sales up a little bit," Blumhoff admitted. However, it wasn't a perfect match. This is because performance metrics drive behaviors. If an engineer needed a little extra cash, they would focus on sales, primarily on the projects they sold, leaving other projects to fall behind.

When Blumhoff stepped in as COO, he analyzed the engineering/sales team and after talking to each person, created a sales department by moving two employees to sales full-time. Each week, the sales team meets to review their sales metrics for the month.

Blumhoff also took sales commissions away from engineering employees but replaced it with a bonus program based on engineering metrics. This aligned better with the goals for the engineering department.

How you pay your employees and how you measure your employees' performance matters. Under Blumhoff's leadership, F.N. Smith's sales team doesn't get paid until the company's been paid. They'll make a sale, but they don't see their commission until the sale is shipped, which incentivizes them to oversee projects and work with engineers. Here's an edited version of our conversation.

IMEC: When deciding which employees would make great full-time sales personnel, what do you look for?

CB: It's the characteristic–how outgoing they are, how easy or comfortable they are speaking to customers, etc. I just observed him [an engineer] interacting with the customer during a machine run off. He built the machine and the customers [were testing] it, and just the natural way he helped identify solutions, the natural way which he made the customer feel at ease. I approached him and said, "Would you like to learn sales?", and he's done a really good job.

IMEC: What's one important hiring piece of advice?

CB: Hire for character, train for skill.

IMEC: A lot of F.N. Smith's business is repeat business, so if your staff is hitting their due dates, they improve their chances of getting more business from those customers. What's the impact of this?

CB: They take a vested interest because they realize it is seven times more expensive to get business from a new customer than it is from an existing customer.

Our customers don't view them as 'salespeople' per say, and a lot of times we've become technical resources because our customers experienced turnover and so they'll call us for history.

IMEC: What about measurable results?

CB: We experienced 10% growth in the first year, whereas the industry average is 5%.

IMEC: You've also set up metrics to monitor performance so if sales start to slip, the sales team reacts right away. How does this work?

CB: I am trying to avoid the silo-ing effect. My sales team does 75% selling, 25% project management. Usually, the project concept starts with the sales team, and then the salespeople, bringing their concept to engineering, and that collaboration between sales and engineering is where they come up with the solution for their client.

IMEC: Share how you've approached sales and marketing.

CB: Sales and marketing are one and the same. We're so small that we wear multiple hats. We're only forty-five employees.

The advantage is they know how to talk the talk with the customers and that's what makes them good at selling. We do really well at walking a factory floor with our customers and solving their problems. So, from the marketing perspective, they know the lingo.

Now we're targeting new customers, but in our current markets. We're sticking with our core competency, whereas four years ago the business strategy was to chase different markets. There is so much potential in our current markets. [F.N. Smith Corporation has expanded into the pet food sub-sector, and now pet food is almost as much of their business as human food!]

Showing customers that it's a team effort now and not a one-person, like the owner, makes a difference. In order for it to be successful, we have to be contributing equally to it as well.

IMEC: What really sets your sales team apart from other sales teams?

CB: It's just the holistic approach [referring to F.N. Smith's strategy of connecting engineering components, the company's technical expertise, and clients]. I'd rather be a trusted advisor for ten years, twenty years, than get a quick sale for the next six months.

FILE UNDER SALES AND MARKETING

F.N. Smith uses a crawl-walk-run strategy to keep current customers engaged and rebuild relationships with previous customers who had lost trust with the company a few years back. Using an awareness campaign, F.N. Smith highlighted its full product line, improved delivery times, and created a better internal quoting process to support customers (some customers of thirty years didn't know the company's full range of products).

Despite popular belief, marketing does not "make things happen." Sales should provide marketing with feedback on what they're hearing. Sales team members may also serve as technical specialists. They've experienced the pains the customer is experiencing, they know what it means to have a down machine, and this allows the sales team to troubleshoot with the customer right away.

Chapter 4

THE MODERN SUPPLY CHAIN AS A COMPETITIVE EDGE

Choose partners who share your values.

In many industries, the pandemic stretched the supply chain beyond reasonable expectations. Yet, we have found creative ways to make it work. In other industries, we have been operating with diminished needs and looking for ways to repurpose and pivot.

There is a groundswell of movement, a robust dialogue relating to the architecture of the modern supply chain. We are collaborating more than ever with engaging partners across industry and functional boundaries to figure this out.

We cannot predict the path for reshoring production–in some industries it can be 60% of the total inventory. We do know that we have to be different and that we have to think globally and execute locally.

There will be some tough decisions ahead. Who will hold the inventory? What is a reasonable safety stock? How many vendors will participate in the network? Exploring what your future supply chain looks like prepares you to compete more fiercely. The other side of this conversation centers around processes you know well, like lean, pull systems, and kanban. Will they go away? Probably not. As business systems become more sophisticated and we collaborate up and down the supply chain, we will gain new insights and find ways to manage inventory and control costs.

Can everything we need be last minute delivery with limited inventory in the supply chain? Again, probably not, and nor should it. Organizations will need to invest in technology, resources, and, potentially, capital to reinforce the supply chain.

Supply chain, that once sleepy topic that rarely gained the same stardom as leadership, operations, or the Madison Avenue glamour of the marketing department, has risen to the top as a predictor of company success. What can we do to leverage our supply chain as a point of strength, a differentiating superpower that emboldens our competitiveness?

We can be more prepared. We can require more reactive capacity in the network. We can seek out strategic partners poised to pivot and provide essential raw materials, parts, and equipment. We can ready ourselves like world class companies do with crisis planning events that test our process for design and capability. We can listen. We can learn. We can take action.

One thing we cannot do, however, is go backwards. Rather, let's take up the courage and fortitude to drive change, think differently, and challenge each other to change paradigms.

Illinois manufacturers, you have achieved the amazing, largely due to supply chain prowess. In this chapter we'll look at the modern supply chain from four different perspectives: redefining the status quo, reinventing for greater confidence, rebalancing using KPIs (key performance indicators), and being crisis-resilient. We will close our conversation with some encouraging words on why supply chain management is making a striking difference for people around the world.

THE MODERN SUPPLY CHAIN: "REDEFINE" STATUS QUO

MIT Senior Lecturer Jonathan Byrns is an author of more than 200 books and articles, with much of his focus on supply chain management and customer-supplier relationships.[26] In this quote, he poignantly drives home the reality: "Many supply chains are perfectly suited to the needs that the business had twenty years ago."[27]

Supply chain is being considered through a fresh, modern lens, largely due to one of the most dramatic global events in our lifetime, the pandemic. We have evolved from supply chain to supply shock to supply resiliency.

Given continued concerns with health care, social distancing, unemployment, the remote workplace, and our economy, it is easy to let the focus on supply chain fall to the bottom.

What's the risk in such an approach? We have learned that we are far more reliable, far more resilient, and far more creative and innovative than we could have even imagined. On several calls discussing the future of the supply chain, we have heard comments from senior level executives sharing comments like: "I'm not sure if I can afford the new supply chain."

But what if we changed the question to: "How can I afford not to change my supply chain model?" We see evidence of why rethinking makes sense. For example, in the food industry, the food service market is struggling as they do not have the ability to immediately shift focus and compete in the retail markets.

Within the circle of supply chain conversation, you will hear terms like reshoring, total cost of ownership, risk management and risk mitigation, reactive capacity, and business continuity planning. Supply chain will be in the spotlight for quite some time, especially on the national and world stage.

Depending on where you are in the supply chain in your industry–raw material provider, distributor, manufacturer, 3PL (third-party logistics), copacker, or other, your approach will vary. Besides the time commitment and resources required, the financial investment in re-engineering your supply chain is a completely valid concern.

Traditionally, we see the total cost of ownership passed down to the consumer, yet buyers will continue to demand low prices. Change will not just impact the supply chain, but how we work. Organizations with large office space, for example, in urban locations are already thinking about future remote work trends. With manufacturers seeking more local labor, costs will rise as manufacturers continue to face the gap between fair living wages and cost containment.

An article in *Harvard Business Review* further underscores why considering the supply chain as status quo will no longer work for manufacturers: "The challenge for companies will be to make their supply chains more resilient without weakening their competitiveness. To meet that challenge, managers should first understand their vulnerabilities and then consider a number of steps—some of which they should have taken long before the pandemic struck."[28]

Consumers, buyers, and regulatory organizations as well as local, state, and federal governments are demanding changes to the supply chain.

Whether you use lean techniques, continuous improvement, process mapping, SWOT, or other tools, unpack and analyze your end-to-end supply chain. Look for opportunities to reduce lead times, improve variability, reduce or eliminate waste, or simplify the process, leveraging your supply chain as a competitive advantage and, thereby, raising it above the status quo.

THE MODERN SUPPLY CHAIN: "REINVENT" TO COMPETE CONFIDENTLY

As the supply chain reacted to the pandemic crisis, we applauded the re-engineering efforts of Illinois manufacturers and answered the call of the health care industry when demand exceeded supply. For some, the pandemic was not the first crisis in their company history. One manufacturer that had operated through the Great Depression and WWII increased production of its ventilators ten times during the pandemic. Another founded in the early 1900s enlisted company retirees to meet production demand of PPE equipment.

There are countless stories like these showing Illinois manufacturers' innovation, creativity, and agile supply chain responding to rapid change. Here are some higher-level lessons on reinventing with confidence:

- Overall inventories are too low. Lean and continuous improvement drives that result, but the statistical models were never designed to address shifts in demand patterns and accelerated replenishment needs.
- The debate continues regarding "offshore" or "outsourcing." This will not change overnight and will create significant challenges when companies look at capital planning, capacity planning, and reinvestment in current domestic assets.
- Flexible, rapid, and responsive will be the KPIs for every future supply chain. KPIs should be measurable. For example, how do you measure flexible and rapid? Product might be shipped before the due date. How do you measure responsiveness? Look to your data for response times. Vendor/supplier selection will now include conversations around "backup" capacity and business continuity planning (BCP).

- Planning tools will get smarter, faster, and more collaborative. The use of shared data and "big data" will become standard for delivering a world class supply chain.
- We need to invest more resources, capital, and technology in the supply chain. It can't be an afterthought because disruptions will happen again and again (you will be so ready for next time, though, after reading this book!).

Beyond normal capacity planning, we hope that manufacturing now includes conversations about how to repurpose assets. Explore production options using your raw materials, WIP (Work-in-Progress), technology/processing, and manufacturing assets.

Supply chain more than deserves a seat at the table.

You are poised to replace old assumptions and business practices. It's exciting to think about your company's organizational potential ability to "reinvent" the supply chain, and, ultimately, compete with greater confidence.

THE MODERN SUPPLY CHAIN: "REBALANCE" USING FIVE POINTS OF DIFFERENCE

The first reaction to a severe supply chain disruption is "organized chaos" and then you attempt to rebalance and update purchasing, replenishment, planning, distribution, and warehouse parameters.

What does a high performing supply chain look like? It has robust planning and replenishment processes, great relationships with vendors and customers, and a versatile sales and operations planning process that keeps you focused on key metrics and trends.

The alternative becomes a day-to-day "redo," placing a manufacturer under constant threat of having the necessary raw materials and supplies to meet production plans and provide product to customers. Herein lies the supply chain as a way to "rebalance," and centralize disconnected systems so customer commitments are met. The goal: create a culture where promises are kept, and customers trust your brand will deliver. Here are five points of difference to consider to enhance your supply chain and strengthen your brand:

1. **Faster:** When speed to market becomes the competitive advantage–the supply chain of tomorrow has to be able to exceed that expectation.
2. **More reliable:** The online-enabled transparency and easy access to a multitude of options regarding where to shop and what to buy drives the competition of supply chains. It's not just the products, it's the shared data and communications that will be part of the future solution. It's also where you will need to capture more information and data, and leverage integrated processes that use optimization.
3. **More accurate:** Accuracy is a companion to moving goods in and out quickly. As orders increase, mistakes are easy to make.
4. **More efficient:** Integrating technology and using "big data" to drive customer engagement is key.

Unlocking efficiencies and capacity by creating or enhancing collaboration from machines to business systems to customers will be the new norm.

5. **More custom**: Customer expectations are growing: the online trend of the last few years has led to increasing service expectations combined with a significant change in order sizes and total number of items. Depending upon your markets, you might see further individualization and customization.

THE MODERN SUPPLY CHAIN: A CHECKLIST

Depending upon your products, customers, and your manufacturing footprint, the crisis in 2020 may have taxed your supply chain to its limits. Here's a checklist to ready your supply chain for any disruption:

- ☐ Consider the role of "big data" relative to sales, markets, products, raw materials, transit times, on-time delivery, shipped in full, and other metrics that help assess the health of your supply chain.
- ☐ Communicate with vendors and providers. Ask them about their business continuity plan (BCP) and their practical ability to supply.
- ☐ Evaluate demand/replenishment needs. Whether you call it a demand forecast, sales plan, operating budget, or distribution requirements, evaluate customer needs over a period of time. This is a version of lean takt time (the rate at which you produce a product to meet customer demand). Whatever you

think the future demand signal should be, it may be completely different. Trust your experience and relationships with customers.

- ☐ Reinvigorate customer relationships and communications. Oftentimes it's not the supply chain group that acquires your product, it's the buyer arm or the procurement group. They may have different KPIs that drive buying behavior.
- ☐ Explore capacity. More than likely the customer demand will exceed your available capacity at the work center and product level. Consider using any and all safety stock available. Consider both replenishment targets and on-hand inventory. At some point, all the safety stock in the "pipeline" will be consumed or "allocated," and you will probably move to first come first serve.
- ☐ Ramp up alternate capacity or less than optimal capacity if possible (alternate tooling/processing is your best friend). Consider establishing contingency plans with major suppliers in advance and reviewing on an annual basis to have something in place. Be creative, think out of the box, and include the shop floor.
- ☐ With raw materials, start with the basics. For example, with PPE, what's the protocol in your industry for usage? Can you get enough PPE to sustain a replenishment plan? What's reusable and what isn't?

- ☐ You can't ship product without packaging materials. What options do you have with vendors? How many alternate vendors do you have approved? Can you ship from another location in the network to the site? There are alternatives to "packaging," like large work-in-process (WIP) containers, paper and plastic (TOTES), and large sacks. Are those viable options for your customer to receive product? In the Consumer Packaged Goods (CPG) space, almost all the product is placed on a shelf, end-of-aisle display or some type of carton shipper or display. Consider substitutions. Will your customer relax packaging requirements, like accepting a plain brown box with a label or item number to speed up replenishment lead time and potentially provide safety stock?
- ☐ If there's one point that carries more weight on your checklist, it is collaborating with your suppliers. Explode the replenishment plan back through your bill of materials and into your vendor's supply chain. Have conversations with vendors about availability, lead times, safety stock, and find out if they are struggling with the same issues.
- ☐ Define your distribution. Have your VOC before making any changes to prevent surprises. Then ask: Where does your product need to be? What are your assumptions about the availability of transportation–IMDL (intermodal is shipping that uses a variety of transportation), truck, ocean, or "last mile"? Can you assume the same transit times in your replenishment model?

- ☐ If your available warehouse space is "tight," you will be challenged. Can you forward deploy any inventory to the customer, the distributor, or a regional distribution center where "last mile" final delivery is a better solution? Not all freight is equal during a crisis. Essential products and supplies are highest priority and therefore earn the highest allocation of available resources. This is just like the freight market and FEMA loads after hurricanes and tornadoes.
- ☐ Regularly review your operational assumptions to ensure you have the operating capacity to replenish based on customer demands. Examine OEE, or Overall Equipment Effectiveness, such as uptime x rate (speed) x material yields regularly. A great plan with bad underlying data will fail every time.
- ☐ Slow moving and obsolete inventory are costly and tie up cash and space. Consider ways to repurpose this inventory into alternate products or markets, or recycle into raw materials.
- ☐ Like any replenishment project plan: Plan–Do–Check–Act. Your supply chain will be "stress tested," and the variability in the demand signal will be off the charts.
- ☐ Stay the course and build a "reasonable" replenishment plan. Clearly define expectations with vendors, providers, customers, and employees.
- ☐ Share day-to-day success stories. Make sure team members see how important their contribution is to the national supply chain.

- ☐ Consider dual sourcing from geographically diverse locations to provide resiliency against future natural or political disruptions from single-sourced suppliers.
- ☐ Ensure that "levers" are installed to respond to changes in holding costs/capital lockup cost if, and when, the current historically low interest rate environment changes. The balance between risk of supply outages and the cost of holding inventory will always be moving, and preparing for that requires companies to develop flexible supply agreements with suppliers and customers.

IMEC wishes to thank Mike Loquercio, Vice President of Supply Chain of Greenleaf Foods, for sharing his expertise on supply chain management in this chapter of Made in Illinois.

THE BIG PLAY: SUPPLY CHAIN OPTIMIZATION

A Conversation with Kim Weninger, Chief Operating Officer
Watchfire Signs in Danville, IL

When you are a small fish in a big pond, you have to be creative to get the resources you need. Supply chain optimization is a subject we discussed with Kim Weninger, the Chief Operating Office of Watchfire Signs. Watchfire Signs is in the electronics industry, which as an industry has exploded within the last few decades. What gives Watchfire Signs a competitive edge is how they handle their supply chain, rather than sitting around and waiting for their supply chain to handle them.

IMEC: What about your supply chain is unique or fierce?

KW: We buy components from all over the world and being somewhat small compared to a lot of other electronics players, we have to be very creative in our sourcing. When things in the electronics' world get tight, we aren't always on the top of the list. So, we have to be very nimble and very resourceful when it comes to our sourcing.

We have multiple qualified components that we can switch out in our printed board assemblies if we need to. We have multiple suppliers we can get them from if we need to. We really pay attention to what's going on in the electronics market and if something looks like it's not going the right way for a certain country, we quickly bring up another supplier in another country.

Also, we have a robust qualification process. We test potential suppliers as well as track component performance. I believe that sets us apart from what others in the industry are doing.

IMEC: So, you avoid putting all your eggs in one basket?

KW: We try to, and most things we do. There are some things where I'm finding we are single sourced on. We're slowly working those into a dual source. Not necessarily a dual source because we might not buy enough of them to have two sources, but we have another one qualified so we can switch if we need to. We run inventory pretty tight, so we have to be careful with that.

One part of our business is electronics. The other part of our business is the fabrication and assembly of the metal. The percentage of our business spent on fabrication and assembly changes every year due to hedging our material. We have a lot of aluminum hedges that we place so we lock in pricing. So far, it's worked out pretty well. For us, predictable is more important than just saving money.

IMEC: So, for those products, you estimate in advance to lock in your pricing?

KW: Yes, and you have to look at the market and see if now is a good time to lock, because what if you lock in and then it goes down two weeks later by a lot? Then you're just locked into the high price.

IMEC: It sounds like your company puts in a lot of research hours. Do you have someone on your team who's responsible for looking at the market and coming up with predictions?

KW: That's part of what our distributor does for us. We do pay a distributor who holds all of our material for us, so we don't have to. Big, big rolls of aluminum, lots of extrusion, stuff like that.

Electronics material goes crazy about every year or year and a half, where there's a huge demand for electronics, which causes the whole industry to be scrambling for parts. Even though everybody doesn't use the exact same component, the materials that go in the components are the same.

IMEC: How do you know it's time to vet another supplier?

KW: Usually it's some kind of data that triggers us. All of a sudden we say, 'Hey, do you realize we're sole sourced on this driver, and if something were to happen, we're in trouble? So, let's start finding another one.' Or it could be, 'Hey, all of a sudden this supplier is not able to meet our demand. What's the reason and what do we have to do to find someone else?' We try to always anticipate those things well in advance.

IMEC: What's involved in qualifying a potential supplier?

KW: It depends on the level of part. If it's a really critical part, it can take three to five months to qualify a supplier. We have someone in Asia who does audits when we have suppliers over there. Then we have to get samples, we have to test those samples, which takes a while, and do prototypes.

IMEC: It sounds expensive for you to vet a supplier and test their parts on a test project. Is that correct, and is it still worth the effort?

KW: Yes, that's why we reserve that process for our most critical quality parts. Not everything goes through that.

IMEC: Was your supply chain disrupted during this past year?

KW: It was, but we were also making less, so they kind of cancelled each other out. I'd say we are seeing more disruption now than we did previously. Some of the raw materials in the world are catching up. That's causing a delay in all the other electronics parts. Also, right now the ports are backed up. Six to nine months after when the original issue was, that's usually when we start to see disruption.

IMEC: Is there another time you can remember something similar to this happening?

KW: Whenever there's a big release in the electronics world because it will suck up a lot of the raw materials for other products.

IMEC: You have been an active member on several boards. Have you ever noticed things that supply chain managers could be doing better? Any advice you would give to another supply chain manager?

KW: I would say not to get comfortable with your supplier because that's usually the biggest mistake I see. They think if they're not, you know, causing a problem, that they could just let it keep sliding, and that's not always true. I think you have to stay on top of their quality, stay on top of how they're doing business-wise. They could be in trouble and you wouldn't know, and then you would be in big trouble because you wouldn't be able to get parts. We always stay on top of this. We have business reviews with our main suppliers.

Also, price check, because things get cheaper and you may still be paying the same. I've been in jobs before where I worked for a big company and then I went to a smaller company and we were paying less for the exact same materials because we paid attention. The bigger company who was buying a lot wasn't paying attention and kept paying higher prices.

IMEC: How often do you have those business reviews with your major suppliers?

KW: We do a quarterly business review with our major ones. We do biannual reviews with the next level down and then an annual review with the next level after that.

IMEC: How long are those?

KW: A quarterly business review could take a day and a half, but that's with our biggest suppliers and we'll go through quality, we will do a tour, usually (when you can travel) we'll go through what the business looks like, any late or quality issues, you name it. They are quite extensive.

The biannual ones are half a day each and then the annual ones are probably two or three hours.

IMEC: I would assume those would need to be longer though, if they're only annual?

KW: They're not the major suppliers, so we don't go into as much detail. You look at a real quick snapshot of if they were late, if there were any quality problems, things like that.

IMEC: Have you ever had an issue where a supplier was misleading you in order to keep your business?

KW: We've had that in the past and that's why I'm saying you have to pay attention and don't get comfortable. We have a lot of key indicators. If any of those are off, we start digging into why. So, if shipments start being late from a supplier that's always on time, we need to know why. We do have formal reviews, and we do have informal ones where we call them up and ask them. In the formal responses, they have to fill out a report, do a presentation, and tell us why the issue occurred. It just depends on what it is.

IMEC: You mentioned data earlier, alerting you if you only have one supplier for a component, and then data again, notifying you when there is a delay or problem with a supplier. It sounds like you're getting data from a lot of different places. Do you have a data management system?

KW: We have an ERP system we use so that as soon as something hits our dock, they scan it and the computer will try to match it up with what the promise date was.

IMEC: Who has access to this data?

KW: We have an MRP system that we developed ourselves. It's on everybody's desktop so you can see everything you need to see there. In fact, the people on the floor use it. We're paperless on our floor, so they pull up the computer, they see what needs to go out, etc., but it pulls from our ERP system. ERPs can be very cumbersome to use and are meant to be used by a professional who does that every day, so we take that data and we put it into a manufacturing system that we made ourselves. It's called Pyro, and we use it for everything.

IMEC: It sounds like things are running pretty smoothly right now, but has there ever been a situation in the past when things were not running smoothly?

KW: We've had quality issues with some of our suppliers and we've learned that we have to implement more incoming quality inspections. When you have a quality problem, sometimes you're forced to make a quick decision to use another product because you don't have a choice. One thing we really learned is to pay attention and up your incoming inspection on really key parts.

IMEC: What did the quality inspection process used to be compared to what it is now?

KW: It used to be a lot more of a visual inspection. Now we have since purchased some equipment, shock chambers, where we actually physically test the parts out of each batch.

That's the problem with electronics, some of the defects

are latent defects. It may test well in the factory, but then it doesn't last, and it breaks pretty quickly, so that's what we try to do with our physical tests. We're going to stress these and if it passes even after stress, then it's good.

IMEC: When you were implementing these new physical tests, how did you know how to go about this? Did you look at best practices, hire an expert to help, etc.?

KW: We kind of do both. We use our supplier because they tell us, 'Here's some tests that we do,' so we copy them. We do have expert labs around the region. And then, we have a full engineering staff, so they give their input as well.

IMEC: Is there anything else that you have implemented in your supply chain that really took it to the next level?

KW: I would say really looking at sourcing and purchasing as two separate departments. That's made a big difference because sourcing is really focused on finding the right source, making sure that they are qualified, all the way from financially qualified to quality qualified. Supplier quality works with sourcing a lot and does a lot of the audits and business reviews, and they're really focused on the quality of the supplier. Purchasing is really focused on making sure we have the materials to build product.

IMEC: So, you're saying they used to be the same department?

KW: Yes, they used to be the same people doing both and

most of the time, making sure we have parts to build our product is going to win and overtake any of the other activities that need to happen.

IMEC: What made you realize you needed to separate the two?

KW: We purchase a lot of components and material. It just depends on what percentage of your product is purchased material. Once you get to the point where it's such a big part of your business, you just have to give it the right attention.

I think what we saw were there were some missed audits and we said, 'Why are you missing these things?' Well, because these same people are too busy making sure we have parts to build product.

Even if you don't have the people to have separate departments, I would mentally keep them separate. These are two separate activities, even if it has to be done by the same person. Here's the sourcing activities you do, and here's the purchasing activities you do. It kind of depends on the size of your company.

IMEC: At least if you look at it separately, the one employee in charge of both can schedule the activities separately on their own personal calendar. 'This part of the day I'm doing purchasing, this part of the day I'm doing sourcing, etc.'

KW: Yes, exactly. Just make sure that you're allowing the time for the sourcing activities. If you look at Stephen Covey's

The 7 Habits of Highly Effective People, he has different quadrants and quadrant two is working on the business. Sourcing is really working on the business. Working in the business is, 'I need parts to build this product. Is it coming on the dock today?

IMEC: Do you have any final advice for other manufacturers?

KW: Just don't get comfortable and pay attention, always.

FILE UNDER SUPPLY CHAIN

"Make a Difference" also translates to helping your organization recognize the importance of the supply chain and what they can do to improve and innovate. As the adage goes, a chain is only as strong as the weakest link. A supply chain brings together the parts, talent, and technology of many companies into the final product delivered on time to exacting customer specifications. There is no need to be the weakest link or to have weak links. Find your strengths and gaps, share your insights and experience, and continue to keep the supply chain at the top of your agenda.

PART 2:
PERFORMANCE

Part 2 is about innovation and operations in making things. Performance is the tactical side of our competitive advantage. We will explore topics like machinery, process, business acumen, and ways to measure our performance so we craft a fierce competitive edge rooted in endurance. You will dive into what sets high performing companies apart with topics like the ten pillars of Industry 4.0, cybersecurity, productivity gaps, robotics, big data, the supply chain as key differentiator, as well as the unsung hero for Illinois manufacturers to compete on the global stage: continuous learning.

Chapter 5

ACHIEVING OPERATIONAL EXCELLENCE

Plan, share, run.

The backstory of Illinois manufacturing is rooted in people who found a way through. They struck a path in the gritty dirt of the Midwest, where early pioneers led a hardscrabble life to work the land and make things with their hands. As an Illinois manufacturer, you blaze your own trails. In this chapter we look at problem-solving and adopting organizational change so you are better positioned to compete globally. While some points may not apply, chances are you will need some of this, somewhere, somehow.

The larger thought is to constantly improve your business by understanding the value of interrelated pieces. There is no silver bullet (much like dieting, fads don't stick). However, there are lessons that our work at IMEC has taught us about approaching problems, efficiencies, and productivity.

Like many of us who are swamped with daily tasks, it is understandable to hear manufacturers talk about the "flavor-of-the-month" in unsympathetic ways. For example, some say *Lean is just another program or they readily admit defeat, saying, We tried lean for a month and it didn't work. Some think Baldrige is "just" a quality award and that quality is not a viable solution.*

But what if we took a more intentional approach to getting the job done on operational efficiency and of making quality really stick? In this chapter, you will learn to leverage operational efficiency as a competitive advantage and explore how to improve your company based on what is right for your goals, industry, and vision. The latter is the ideal prompt for giving Baldrige a seat at the table on the topic of operations. The two big questions this excellence framework brings to the discussion are:

- How do you design, manage, and improve your key products and work processes?
- How do you ensure effective management of your operations?

The goal is not to make products cheaper, faster, or feature-rich. Global competitors build strength, just like an elite athlete commits to mastering various areas of their training regime. Strong companies lean into their power centers and compensate for their weaknesses by listening to customers, taking action on continuous improvements, and charting a course for organizational success.

CIRCUMSTANCES: THE FAST TRAIN TO CHANGE MANAGEMENT

So-called "traditional" organizational models, where silos, structure, and hierarchy abound and where resistance to change is prevalent, are in for a rough road. Beyond a crisis, there is always a major turning point. At that juncture, we will need to seek answers to questions like:

- How do we become more agile, forward-thinking, and proactive?
- How do we sustain an ability to adapt quickly and efficiently to unforeseen circumstances?
- How do we build a resilient culture?

We might believe challenge requires the ability to predict future challenges better or improve the organization's ability to work remotely or even shore up supply chains. Of course, all of the above are important. However, the real issue is the mentality of leadership.

When it comes to change, leadership is inherently slow to embrace it. This isn't odd or heartless. Rather, it's human nature to resist change. Called cognitive bias, we cling to our "belief systems" like a life preserver (fun fact: compared to humans, monkeys are much more open to adopting new strategies if it means greater efficiency).[29]

When push comes to shove, it's another matter. Crisis is a catalyst to taking action because a catastrophe is urgency at its highest point. In this spot, leaders sometimes feel they have no or few options. However, you have multiple opportunities to make simple but significant changes which can put you in a better position to weather a storm if you embrace change as an opportunity to improve.

We can all do better when it comes to change management. We can use our corporate courage to embrace change before it is foisted upon us. We can be more open to new ideas and forward-thinking behaviors. We can foster inclusiveness, cross-train employees, and empower them to make better decisions faster. We can create a resilient culture where people think on their feet and are always looking for a smarter way to do things.

Here's the challenge: examine your organizational culture and think about how you will transform your company to be more adaptive, rather than embracing the status quo because it's familiar. Change will come one way or another. It's much easier to handle it if you're primed (or, evidently, a primate!) for it.

A HUMOROUS LOOK AT THE COMMON PITFALLS OF PROBLEM-SOLVING

In most manufacturing companies, problem-solving is in high demand. This becomes particularly apparent whilst pursuing a continuous improvement journey. It won't be a stretch to say that all continuous improvement tools/practices are built around some form of problem-solving. Ironically, many of these companies have devoted time and resources to the task of training their associates with success as elusive as the missing pair of scissors that purportedly keeps floating around the plant floor.

We thought we would give you a brief rest from the more serious tone thus far in *Made in Illinois.* Here are common lessons we've learned from deploying problem-solving across many companies, presented with a touch of humor for good measure:

1. **What problem?** Like an ostrich burying its head in the sand, it's easy to pretend that a problem didn't occur. Why do we do this? There are many reasons but typically it means we have chosen the path of "We don't have time to work on this." R*eframing problems as opportunities can make a difference (unless you're an ostrich, in which case, there is no problem).*
2. **Treat symptom versus root cause.** Symptoms must be treated, but only dealing with symptoms will rarely solve the actual problem. Of course, we know this, but it's easier to grab an aspirin than do yoga to reduce the stress. In manufacturing, "symptoms" are treated by the ubiquitous availability of "over-the-counter" remedies: duct tape, shims, hammers, and the like. (OK, we can all agree that duct tape really is the go-to solution for homeowners and makers everywhere, right?). Needless to add, we will spend much more time and resources once the problem overwhelms the temporary solution. *"Pay me now" is always better than "pay me a lot later."*
3. **Try to solve "big" problems.** Every business has small problems and large ones. Rather frequently

though, unsolved, small problems end up becoming big problems. Associates are made to feel like heroes for taking on big problems. No matter the person's skill, big problems are, quite simply, difficult to solve. *End world hunger, indeed. Rewarding employees who go above and beyond to solve said small problems before they become big ones might encourage more problem-solving (hint, hint: David, we like Starbucks!!!).*

4. **Solution looking for a problem.** As human beings, we have many shortcomings, but one of the most insidious ones in problem-solving is our attachment to a prior conclusion. This really comes down to the lack of willingness to meet the problem where it is or even banking a genius idea just because it's not needed at the moment. We withdraw to the comfort of our prior conclusion, our preconceived solution, no matter what the problem is. *To a hammer, everything looks like a nail.*
5. **Opinion versus fact-based approach.** Everyone is entitled to their opinion. Yes, everyone. The dictionary definition of opinion: *a judgment one holds as true.* While solving a problem, whose opinion do we go with? The best approach is to treat the problem as a person and go with his/her opinion. The good news is that Mr. or Ms. Problem is built on facts versus opinion. *In God We Trust, everyone else bring data.*
6. **What problem are we working on?** This is a subtle, but an often-overlooked pitfall. We find ourselves

trying to solve "something." (Hello, problem, are you there? Hello? It's me, Solution.) But we clearly have not thought about what problem, exactly, it is that we are working on. We may fix something but not the real problem. *Work on everything,* all at once.

7. **Blame someone first.** The joke is that the first step in problem-solving is to blame someone, first. (Hmmm . . . where have we seen this exchange before? With our siblings–still salty about your sister stealing that concert tee, aren't you?) Needless to add, the face in front of the thumb feels miserable, but the worst thing about this in problem-solving is: that exact person may hold the key to opening the problem-solving door. And, what do you expect with future problems? Look under the carpet. *If the business is serious about continuous improvement culture, please don't let Whodunit happen.*
8. **Avoiding the one closest to the problem.** Not everyone is a Sherlock Holmes, someone adept at piecing together the murder scene in their minds. Why do businesses ask "someone else" to solve problems? It is a lack of empowerment. Frontline associates are supposed to keep doing whatever they are always doing, except problem-solving because there are other experts for that. *Problems don't respect title.*
9. **Vague problem descriptions.** Why do we accept problem statements like, *"It doesn't work" or "Short of parts?"* Dr. Edward Deming gave us the PDCA

(Plan-Do-Check-Act) cycle. While there is profound philosophy behind this, there may be a check-the-box mindset in play while applying this. A more effective description would be *Plan-Plan-Plan-Plan-Plan-Do-Check-Act! We interrupt your reading pleasure with a commercial break from Albert Einstein: "Formulation of a problem is often far more essential than its solution, which may be merely a matter of mathematical or experimental skill."*

10. **Not systematic/scientific approach.** Rather frequently companies, notably management, demand swift action when facing a problem. *Swift, I tell you!* Well, there is nothing wrong with a bias for action but what often results is "cutting corners" in the rank and file. Of all things needed to foster a problem-solving culture, training is right up there. Socratic questioning works best! *The reason is simple: the problem is usually smarter than us and will always win over shortcuts.*

Reflection on these pitfalls reveals a nugget of wisdom: what matters more than the problem itself is the human condition, specifically the mindset with which we approach problem-solving. Being aware of these pitfalls allows us to better utilize the many problem-solving tools, methods, and practices that are readily available out there–all while keeping our sense of humor intact.

ROOT CAUSE ANALYSIS AS AN ESSENTIAL SKILL

Drilling down to the atomic level of a problem isn't always easy, but it pays big dividends in saving time, aggravation, and costs. Let's take the pandemic as an example. Face masks, proper hand washing, and social distancing are all countermeasures to keep people from catching the virus and spreading it. We see the "flattening of the infection curve" as a result. Yet, at this point, these measures only treat the problem's symptoms.

Switching gears, what about the common problems we face as manufacturers? Supply shortages, quality failures, and design shortcomings to name a few. How much do they cost your business? Do we stop and ask ourselves if we are working on the symptoms or the causes of those problems? What would be the cost avoided if we had addressed the root cause? What do we need to learn in order to find the root cause? What experiments do we plan to run? What data are we going to collect? Just like with a global pandemic crisis, the costs of containment are always disproportionately high relative to avoiding the problem altogether.

The importance of root cause problem-solving cannot be underscored enough. Consider these questions:

- How do you rate your team's abilities when it comes to this skill?
- How well does your team solve problems at the root cause level?
- What approach do you take? What training has been provided?
- Can your team create a robust problem statement to start the problem-solving process?

CONTINUOUS QUALITY IMPROVEMENT: LEAN AND SIX SIGMA

Over the years, operating and management strategies have taken on new names, new packaging, and even become their own "fads" within industries. Who can forget Quality Circles in the late 70s or Total Quality Management (TQM) in the 1980s? Today, there's Total Productive Maintenance (TPM), Toyota Production System (TPS), lean manufacturing (a methodology to reduce waste and make processes more efficient), Six Sigma (a systematic approach to enhance quality and reduce variability in processes), Training Within Industry (TWI), and value engineering (a systematic method of designing for the highest possible value at the lowest possible cost). There's ISO, TS, QS, AS 9100. There's Statistical Process Control (SPC), Production Part Approval Process (PPAP), Advanced Product Quality Planning (APQP), fishbones, paretos, scatters, and hundreds more.

Regardless of what you call them or what buzzwords are attached, most companies want to deliver products of impeccable quality, on time, at costs that will generate the highest profit margins. If the pursuit of these goals is viewed as a short-term strategy, with a defined life span, it doesn't fit the most appropriate and impactful name of all: continuous improvement.

Many companies admit their lean manufacturing deployments are stalled. Some leaders say they've done "all that they can." Still, others have invested considerable dollars and time in a continuous improvement methodology (Six Sigma, for instance) but are not seeing the return on their investment.

Integrating lean manufacturing and Six Sigma (and other continuous improvement strategies) is actually a simple concept. If you consider all the tools both methods have to offer, and you select the right tool for the task at hand, it really doesn't matter what you call your strategy . . . as long as you have one.

Get the best out of both methods. By integrating lean and Six Sigma, companies are able to tackle problems more effectively. Simply put, lean tools are a good choice for eliminating waste. Six Sigma works best when a company needs to tackle a specific problem and minimize variation in a process.

The processes, however, are not mutually exclusive. In fact, if you deploy Six Sigma alone, you may end up spending months fixing a process that in itself could be wasteful. Conversely, if you only implement Lean, you may never get to the root cause of specific problems that, if corrected, could transform your quality or cost structures. By combining lean and Six Sigma you have the opportunity to:

- Address all key processes
- Seamlessly integrate waste removal, time and variability reduction, and increased productivity
- Deliver products more quickly with exceptional quality
- Impact business improvements rapidly
- Achieve a competitive edge in the market

Where to begin. When trying to rationalize the two approaches, think of it this way: When you build a home, you have a blueprint. Each project calls for a specific set of tools and guidelines to ensure that sections of the structure are being built with utmost quality and safety. Yet, at the same time, you are following a process to build the home in the most timely and cost effective fashion.

The same analogy is true in your business. You can't select your tools until you have a defined set of objectives for your projects. Value Stream Mapping (more on this in a bit, we promise!) is one of the foundations of a lean enterprise. It allows you to look at every step in the operational process and identify the actions that do and do not add value to the end customer. Using this roadmap, you're able to identify performance gaps, define improvement projects, charter improvement teams, and select the right tools for closing the gaps. One such tool might be Six Sigma.

Too often, companies see lean and Six Sigma as distinctly different initiatives. Without integrating the two programs, these implementations can compete for resources and end up limiting the success of either. IMEC advocates using a unified approach to conserve valuable company resources and achieve maximum results at a more rapid rate.

FIVE LEAN, PRODUCTIVITY-BOOSTING TOOLS FOR MANUFACTURERS

Lean manufacturing uses many lean tools to improve production and efficiency by getting the most out of each resource. The goal of lean manufacturing is to find better ways to do things–requiring less effort, less time, and fewer resources.

Some lean tools may be more appropriate for one business than another. Apply only those that will most effectively meet the needs of the issue you are trying to resolve. Currently, in our experience, Value Stream Mapping (Manufacturing and Transactional), 5S, Kanban, Kaizen, and Focus PDCA are among the most useful lean tools around.

Value Stream Mapping. Value Stream Mapping (VSM) is a visual lean diagnostic tool that helps organizations optimize manufacturing and production. Mapping helps to build the roadmap to the ideal future state.

Value stream maps are typically used to analyze the current process, highlight problems, and develop solutions for a system-wide change. As the name suggests, VSM provides a visual aid or map that helps participants understand the current problems by:

- Displaying the interaction between all items within the process.
- Bringing secondary items to the forefront (like scheduling, department workflow, and material management).
- Visually representing information and material flow throughout the process.
- All being done typically in a single document that is easy to read and understand.

By visually mapping the relationships of all items within a process, potential problems and losses (wasted time, resources, or materials) are easier to identify.

Potential solutions become clear. As the process continues, solutions are visually represented in a manner that allows all parties to understand the impact or change to the original process. A system-wide process change can then be implemented much more effectively.

Through the VSM life cycle, all new or updated processes are represented by an updated visual map or otherwise known as a future state map, which allows the process of improvement to continue. Because this lean tool supports continuous improvements, it can be used in support of Kaizen (we'll be talking more about VSM in the next section so stay tuned!).

5S–Workplace Organization. The 5S system is designed to improve efficiency through a systematic approach to organization and cleanliness in the workplace. The system includes five fundamental guidelines (five S's) that help improve workplace efficiency. The five S's are: sort, set, shine, standardize, and sustain. In practice, 5S makes workplaces more efficient and effective by:

- Removing unneeded items from each work area (Sort).
- Arranging each unique work area to maximize efficiency (Set).
- Cleaning each work area after every shift to help find and eliminate issues before they become major problems (Shine).

- Documenting improvements so they can be more easily applied in other work areas, as well as being used to bring new personnel up to speed quicker (Standardize).
- Making sure each step is repeated to ensure continuous improvement (Sustain).

(NOTE: The most difficult part of making a 5S program work is sustaining what was done in the first four S's. Lacking the discipline to sustain leads to the failure of many of these programs.)

As a lean tool, 5S is used in many industries, including manufacturing, software, and health care. It can be one of the easiest lean tools to start with, and it can be used with Kaizen and Kanban to create the most efficient workplace possible.

The concept of 5S revolves around the biggest S of all: Safety. As such, you may hear it called 6S in many cases.

Kanban. Kanban is a visual production system in which a supply of parts is delivered to the production line as needed, increasing efficiency. This lean tool works by making sure that workers have what they need, where they need it, and when they need it.

Historically, employees used Kanban cards to signal when they needed more parts, and new parts were not delivered until there was a card signaling a demand for new parts. More recently, physical Kanban cards are being replaced by a system that electronically signals demand, using specialized software. More commonly known as E-Kanban, the system can automatically request new parts using a series of barcodes that are scanned to signal when new parts are needed.

Using Kanban, employers can more easily manage inventory and reduce unneeded stock, focusing instead on the items that need to be stockpiled. In turn, facilities can react to actual needs, rather than making guesses to anticipate the future, reducing waste, and improving efficiency.

Kaizen. Dating back to World War II, *Kaizen* is a Japanese word that translates to "change for the good" and was used to rebuild after the war.

When used correctly, this lean tool fosters continuous improvement in quality, technology, processes, productivity, company culture, and safety. Kaizen leverages knowledge and ingenuity from every employee, from upper management to the cleaning crew. As a result, suggestions for improvement come from every area of the business: production, procurement, management, logistics, finance, and so on. In most cases, individual improvements do not lead to major changes by themselves; rather, a continuous stream of small changes leads to major improvements in productivity, safety, and effectiveness while reducing waste.

A more modern use of Kaizen is to plan events, commonly known as Kaizen events. The APICS Dictionary defines a kaizen event as the "implementation arm of a lean manufacturing program" and notes that events typically are carried out in one week. In other words, it is all about action.

Kaizen events are official activities designed to create rapid change in the workplace. Used in support of the Kaizen process, these events target specific areas that need to be improved. Intense effort is then spent until the targeted area has been improved, usually over the span of one or two weeks. This approach is especially useful in getting people on board with Kaizen because it results in dramatic changes in a short period of time. Kaizen events should be used to support the overall Kaizen process.

Companies that practice Kaizen develop a culture in which employees feel empowered to make suggestions anywhere improvements can be made, whether in their own department or elsewhere.

Kanban is entwined with Kaizen in that teams and individuals are encouraged to participate in continuously improving Kanban solutions and overall production processes. Kaizen, Kanban and 5S are all lean tools that can be implemented together.

Focus Plan-Do-Check-Act (PDCA). Focus PDCA is an organized, logical approach to improving business processes. This lean tool's strength comes from its clear, no-nonsense steps. The purpose of Focus PDCA is to provide a structure that guides the process of problem-solving and process improvement. This approach establishes a comprehensive analysis, response, action plan, and feedback loop to ensure success.

A CLOSER LOOK AT VALUE STREAM MAPPING AS AN INTERNAL COMPETITIVE INTELLIGENCE TOOL

If you are a continuous improvement leader, Value Stream Mapping (VSM) most likely ranks as your favorite pail and shovel in the sandbox. While we touched on VSM in the previous section, let's explore, play and create with it more in-depth here.

What VSM is not: VSM is not observing and documenting an individual doing their work. This is a work study, and a work study may result as an action from a VSM, but VSM is meant to span multiple functions and workstations.

What VSM shouldn't be: A VSM should not be a team of one collecting data to fill in the blanks. While it may technically be a VSM, there is little benefit from this. The benefit comes from collaboration, discussion, arguments, and sharing of ideas that can only come about in a team environment. VSM is the format that provides focus for this teamwork.

Why is it useful? Where does it fit in your lean journey?

It's hard to imagine an organization not finding benefit in using VSM. It is a flexible, easy-to-use diagnostic tool that does a tremendous job of representing a process from start to finish. It's visual, easy for most people to follow and understand, and promotes focused discussion, brainstorming, and problem-solving among a diverse group of participants. It has been used successfully in manufacturing, health care, banking and financial services, insurance, education, non-profits, and many more industries.

When starting a lean journey, VSM should be one of the first activities taken. Prior to VSM or any other lean initiative, it is a good idea to set up a lean steering committee or another guidance entity for management support and direction. This will help focus lean efforts on issues and opportunities that will have the most impact on the business. The lean steering committee will help direct which product families to focus on first, allocate resources, set scope and boundaries and will be a sounding board for suggestions resulting from the VSM.

VSM allows a team to see the big picture and focus on what will have the most impact on the entire value stream. For example, without VSM, a business may focus on improving productivity of a non-bottleneck machine. A more impactful solution would be to reduce setup time on a primary piece of equipment which currently drives a very large batch size and excess inventory (and lead time) throughout the process.

If a business has limited lean exposure, it is a good idea to precede VSM with an introduction to lean processes via educational workshops, a book club, and tours of other lean businesses. At minimum, you want to have the VSM core team familiar with value-add, non-value-add, eight wastes, and lean tools like SMED, 5S, cellular, among others.

You don't have to start with VSM. You can start with 5S in your lean journey. It is easy for everyone to comprehend; it allows for mass participation and it's a foundation for many other lean tools. It drives discipline (if it's not already there), and the results are immediately noticeable and often dramatic. Both 5S and VSM can be done in parallel but should be tools used early in your lean journey. A VSM may help determine which areas to focus your 5S efforts on.

VSM itself does not improve anything; it is a diagnostic

tool. The goal of VSM is to implement a future state with less waste. VSM without implementation yields nothing. We need to use VSM to determine our roadmap and the projects, activities, and policy changes that must be put in place to achieve our improvements. VSM is great for analyzing and planning, but it is simply that–putting a plan together. The benefit comes from being able to make changes through the understanding, vision, and consensus developed in the VSM.

PREVENTATIVE MAINTENANCE NOW FOR SUCCESS LATER

In times of uncertainty, we focus on the things we can control. When facing a slowdown in incoming orders, employee absenteeism, or nagging equipment issues, companies can feel greater confidence if they are prepared. As with any project, following a structured procedure is key. Follow the steps below to ensure an efficient and productive project.

Scope. What machinery is the most critical? What machinery has had the lowest Overall Equipment Effectiveness (OEE) over the last quarter? Go back through old Preventative Maintenance (PM) sheets or work orders to determine where your time is best spent. Answers to questions on timeline, affected equipment/departments, and budget need to be finalized here before the planning can take place. A clearly defined scope is paramount in avoiding scope creep.

Planning and Preparation. The planning and preparation step of any project is always the most important step but often it is overlooked or hurried through. There are several areas to consider in this step; below are just a few:

- *Workforce:* How many workers do you need? Do they have the necessary skills?
- *Resources:* What tools, equipment, or third-party resources are needed?
- *Logistics:* Will you have what you need, when you need it?
- *Materials:* Are raw materials or spare parts on hand?
- *Safety:* Have all hazards been identified? Are workers aware of those hazards?

The more time you spend working through these areas, the less likely you will be surprised when the work gets started. Murphy's Law says that anything that can go wrong will go wrong, so have contingency plans ready when roadblocks arise.

Execution. Now that you have planned the work, it's time to work the plan. Don't be surprised if unforeseen issues come up during the work. If you've spent adequate time preparing, these should be minimal. Once work wraps up, be sure to conduct a final inspection before handing off equipment.

Startup and Evaluation. Once final inspections are complete and the project lead has signed off, you can begin to bring the equipment back online. Start slow and check for part fitment, new or concerning noises, or vibrations. It's always best to have a representative from operations present since they tend to spend the most time around the equipment. When everyone is satisfied with the operation, take time to bring the team together to capture successes and opportunities to improve, and always document those for consideration in future projects.

A TOOL TO MEASURE OPERATIONAL PERFORMANCE: THE DASHBOARD

A dashboard sounds so very simple. Everybody uses dashboards in business these days, but do they really impact success? Understanding the origin of the word "dashboard" might help, as the term actually hails from manufacturing.

Back in the day, carriage makers built a "dashboard" so mud and rocks would not "dash" up from horses' hooves. In the early 1900s, carriages went the way of modern companies like Blockbuster (does anyone else miss those trips to the video store?), and dashboards became the place for speedometers, gas gauges, and other instruments (progress marches forward).[30]

Most of us were using dashboards before we started working. We look at them all the time when we are driving our cars and don't really think too much about them. Why is that? Because they are very easy to use and tell us quickly when we need to make a correction or solve a problem.

What goes into a dashboard?

First, there are the must-have gauges and dials and digital signals that we use throughout our drive: speedometer, gas gauge, temperature gauge, oil pressure gauge and voltmeter. These are the few key pieces of information we need to know on a regular basis to keep us on track. This way we know when we need to speed up and slow down, when we need to add gas, and whether or not the car's lubrication, temperature control and electrical systems are working properly. If you apply that to business needs, figure out how to measure how quickly or slowly you are addressing client needs (your speedometer), when to replenish or enhance assets (your fuel gauge), and how to keep the organization in good shape by regularly maintaining assets (your oil pressure, temperature and electrical gauges).

The assets you are concerned about might be both physical assets and people assets. These three dashboard gauges in the car make corrections on shorter intervals. So, ask yourself what key indicators do you need to review on a regular basis to keep your enterprise running smoothly, at the right speed? Where do you have the agility to make quick corrections?

How do dashboards alert us to problems up ahead?

Next are the indicator lights or sounds that indicate a real problem. A car makes a sound and flashes an indicator light when there is a problem with the battery, the engine, the lubrication system, or the tires. When you hear these sounds and see the indicator come on, you know you have a problem that must be addressed immediately. Sometimes you need to get additional data by looking at the message page to find out how low a tire is; or, you may need to take it somewhere to have the car's computer analyzed to better understand more about the specific problem.

Applying this second set of indicators into a business setting, decide what indicators will help you determine when it's time for special action plans or corrective action teams. What are the signals that tell you that you have a significant problem to be addressed with a higher level of resources? If it is bigger than a simple correction of moving the gas pedal up or down, you need a team who understands the problem and can put in place some larger corrective actions to get your car back on the road.

How to avoid dashboard distractions.

Lastly, we have quite a few gauges and indicators that we may not use often, or maybe we don't use at all. Think of this as all that other data that we may not need to use on a regular basis, but we might refer to it from time to time. On our car's dashboard, the outside temperature gauge reveals when the temperatures are dropping. A compass indicates direction if you get a bit turned around. Most of us have a lot of data that we just look at every now and then to make sure nothing unusual is going on in our businesses. This data, while interesting, may not be the best data to put on your dashboard. It might end up distracting you from day-to-day management.

So, the next time you want to put a dashboard together for your business, try sitting in your car. Think about the gauges and indicators you need to keep that complex machine operating correctly. Then, really think about identifying the key data that will help you make good decisions and modifications to keep your enterprise running smoothly.

(More on this later when we talk about big data and how dashboards are changing the way we evaluate performance within a manufacturing company.)

THE SIMPLE TRUTH ABOUT OPERATIONAL EXCELLENCE

If you are running a business with defined goals, you are much more likely to achieve them with a strategic plan of action. When people within your organization connect their contribution with the big vision, real excellence becomes possible.

We have guided many manufacturers to train and develop their team to pursue performance excellence. One key area is personal productivity. In the personal productivity development process, we help participants define their personal and professional vision, mission, and goals with support from a designated mentor. Here's what they learn.

Detailed goals are SMART goals:

- Specific
- Measurable
- Achievable
- Realistic
- Tangible

These goals include dates, actions, and measures. In addition, they are aligned with organizational metrics and objectives to ensure success.

As part of the goal process, consider your value to the

organization down to the minute value of your time. This will reveal habits or activities that are obstacles to your goals. Discover your High Payoff Activities (HPAs) which will ensure that daily activities are in line with goals. As you analyze your time, what are the things that deliver maximum value in your work and at home? What are the things that take up time, but don't add much value?

Participants often uncover some faulty beliefs about time, activity, and the personal "stories" we tell ourselves which limit our goal achievement (like "I can't do this because . . ." or "I'm not experienced enough to do this . . ."). They have accountability discussions with their mentors, coaches, and fellow team members to report on their goals regularly.

Work and habit changes do not come easily. Measurement and accountability to yourself and others is hard to face every day. Staying task-driven can be difficult. Yet, through each lesson the team will become more results-driven, see personal and professional break-throughs, and achieve goals that may have felt unattainable not so long ago.

THE BIG PLAY: COLLABORATION

A Conversation with Lucas Derry, President-Owner Header Die and Tool in Rockford, IL

IMEC spoke with Lucas Derry, the president and owner of Header Die and Tool, a global supplier of cold forming tooling and other specialty manufactured parts. Header Die and Tool has a team of approximately fifty employees and a commitment to continuous improvement with an emphasis on communication and collaboration. These qualities allow the company to have a system in place to pass the manual skills down to a new generation of workers and ensure that all generations on the team are working together. By collaborating and playing off each other's skills, they improve processes and make an even better product.

An employee of the younger generation may have an idea on how to use CAD/CAM to integrate more tool libraries, while an employee who has been there for several years knows the ins and outs of the company and little tips they have picked up that aren't written down. Together, they can create a process that integrates technology, makes life easier on employees, and includes the learned knowledge of a seasoned professional at Header.

After much work, most of Header's employees see the bigger picture and understand how these partnerships better the company and employees. Employees who are going to be retiring in the next five years can transfer their knowledge to a newer employee and help the employee be successful.

This is something Derry had been thinking about since

he began his career with Header at the age of twenty-five. At the time, Derry was the youngest employee at the company. When he looked around, he was aware that if nothing changed, the other employees would all retire and take their knowledge with them. They needed to begin training people and hiring new talent to ensure that the company remained successful through the generations.

Derry shared his views on the qualities necessary to be a stronger competitor.

IMEC: How do you view global competitiveness?

LD: To be globally competitive, you [need to have] an engaged workforce. Is everyone going to come in all day, every day and just want to win-win-win? No, not necessarily, but for the most part, your team has to be engaged. They have to be working for something that is bigger than themselves.

IMEC: So how does Header Die and Tool, a small, Illinois manufacturer, keep its workforce engaged and stay globally competitive?

LD: Team Involvement. Header isn't afraid to get their whole team involved, even though it took a little while for our team to adjust to the new culture. It's not uncommon here for leadership to ask their frontline employees, 'Hey, how can we do this better?'

IMEC: Can you give us an example?

LD: Asking something as simple as where they want to put

the new piece of equipment instead of management deciding where it goes. I'll say: 'Guys, I don't ask you to come layout my office. You're the ones using this stuff. So, what would work for you?' Asking for input has had a huge effect on our workforce.

IMEC: That's all great, but it's not enough to ask your team for their input. How do you follow through with their recommendations?

LD: If it's safe, if it works, if it flows better–let's do that.

IMEC: Header used to have machines in neat, orderly rows. Employees said this layout, though it looked organized, wasn't functional. Now you group machines where certain machines will be surrounding a central machine. Why is this?

LD: It functions much better for the employees on the floor, and it is just one example of how employee insight led to a more productive and happier work environment.

IMEC: How would you rate your overall employee morale right now?

LD: If I were to rate it right now, I would probably give it about an 8.5. Things can always be better, but I think our team is aware of it and trying to make improvements to make things better. We don't have fifty cheerleaders, but we probably have fifty people that are at least rooting for the same team.

IMEC: How important is collaboration, especially with a diverse range of ages?

LD: The whole team must work together. A sales team can be very good and bring many opportunities, but they need the machinists who can make the orders. On the flipside, the machinists can be very skilled, but they need the sales team to bring in the orders, otherwise they have nothing to make. Having people here who are in their early to mid-60s to people who are in their early 20s . . . they think differently, they have different values, they find different things important in a workforce.

IMEC: Succession planning is important for many small to midsize manufacturers. How do you view it?

LD: Succession is not just on a leadership level . . . it's on a level of manufacturing as well. [Header Die and Tool's workforce is made up of machinists, but also hands-on, craftsman type skills.] It's an art, and it's not something a machine can do. The team understands without bringing in new talent, without training new people . . . the company can't be successful. If the company is not going to be successful, [the workforce] won't be successful, and they have embraced that.

IMEC: What about the role of accountability?

LD: To be competitive, a company needs to know how they are operating and where people's roles and responsibilities are. One thing that makes Header somewhat unique is the fact that we do quarterly sit-downs with our team and review the performance of the organization and how they play a role. And for, you know, a small, privately-held company, to have our team understand a) if you're profitable and b) how they can contribute to profit, sets us apart.

IMEC: Does hiring for cultural fit tie in with employee accountability as well and how does Header's hiring strategy play a role in your company culture?

LD: There are risks to hiring, and not every new employee Header has hired has worked out. One reason a new employee may not work out is if they don't fit the company culture.

Part of keeping a good culture and keeping people, you know, wanting to be accountable and driven, is making sure that those people that don't fit that . . . we really don't have a place for them.

IMEC: Do you think that to have a good workforce culture, you need a large, dedicated human resources department?

LD: You don't need a huge human resources department. This is what's important to the company, we need you onboard, what resources can we give you to help you do your job better?

IMEC: What last piece of advice would you give to another small manufacturer?

LD: I believe in culture and sharing things because at the end of the day, the company is a lot more successful because of it.

FILE UNDER COLLABORATION

Derry shared the story about a new salesperson who was excited to learn but eager to get out and sell. One tip Derry gave him was to visit the factory floor and get to know the manufacturing employees. There is no "Us Versus Them" at Header anymore, which actually was part of the culture when Derry started his career there at age twenty-five. Each person's role is connected to another person's role, and the sum total is a commitment to collaboration.

In 2020, Derry focused on improving accountability throughout the organization. Most employees responded positively because they have an attitude where they want to "win." Other employees felt like accountability measures put extra pressure on them. While that may not necessarily be a bad thing, the best is when employees aim to "kick butt and take names" every day as Derry so aptly summed it up.

Chapter 6

INTEGRATING TECHNOLOGY FOR GREATER PROCESS INNOVATION

You've got gold. You've got data.

Technology may be the single greatest challenge and opportunity for the manufacturing industry. It has evolved and changed how manufacturers—especially small and midsize manufacturers—operate their businesses, in ways that even a few years ago didn't seem possible.

The physical and cyber-based systems that run today's intelligent factories and supply chains are increasingly interconnected. Through advanced networking and computing technologies, production capabilities far exceed what was possible in previous generations. Manufacturing's digitization is only going to increase.

We have learned that technology-related challenges aren't what is keeping business owners awake at night—it's who will do the work and how to train them.

For the past decade, the Manufacturing Extension Partnership (MEP) National Network has annually surveyed thousands of its US manufacturing clients to identify top challenges. This data is a pulse check on manufacturing and helps us better understand what is critically important to business owners and CEOs.

Employee recruitment and retention are glaring outliers in our data. Manufacturing company CEOs and owners are increasingly concerned about the future of their workforce. MEP clients reporting this as a challenge have more than doubled, and it is now the second most frequently reported challenge.

Some challenges for MEP clients have remained consistent over the past ten years, such as continuous improvement. Other issues have become increasingly important. Chief among them is technology.

While US manufacturing is entering a new era of opportunity, the industry is still grappling with the speed of technological change, increased customer demand for more customized products, and the ability to provide real-time information. With the intersection of these challenges comes the need for a workforce to seamlessly deliver quality products that meet evolving customer needs in a globally competitive market. This will continue to define how opportunities are realized and challenges are overcome.

Industry evolution and advancement should not mask

the everyday challenges US manufacturers face, and instead should help solve some of these challenges. This response is already seen with the growth of smart interfaces, cobots, and virtual/augmented reality. Each of these technological advancements can help focus the training needed for the workforce of tomorrow.

Illinois manufacturers are taming the Wild West once again when it comes to technology. In this chapter, we will pioneer this new territory together with hope and positive anticipation. Sorting out the many options is not easy. Helping manufacturers make a wise investment in the technology they choose, however, is something we do every day. Here are the questions we suggest starting with: *How will I build the smart factory? Will using technology save me money? Will I be able to expand production and capacity with technology? Can I afford the investment? Why do I care about Industry 4.0? How will I leverage the smart factory, IoT, data, technology innovation on the shop floor, SEO, sensor technology, cloud technology, and the SaaS model (especially when depreciating capital)?*

As manufacturers, we love new toys, no doubt. Yet, what will we commit to improving the organization and our global competitiveness? Many small to midsize manufacturers do not have CIOs or CTOs and are falling behind in the adoption of new tech–they need more visibility into what is happening around the world. Without further delay, let's explore these challenges together...

IMEC wishes to thank Nico Thomas, Performance Analyst for the Program Evaluation and Economic Research of NIST's Manufacturing Extension Program for his contributing remarks to this chapter introduction of Made in Illinois.

THE GREAT ROBOTS VS. JOBS DEBATE AND THE TEN PILLARS OF INDUSTRY 4.0

There is a confusing barrage of articles and opinions on Industry 4.0 (in a nutshell, the digitization of manufacturing). Some pundits create new terms, others provide competing definitions around similar concepts, and others seek proven case studies to justify new technologies. Still others are already talking about Industry 5.0 while 4.0 remains in ill-defined infancy.

So how do we define Industry 4.0? One commonly accepted attribute of Industry 4.0 is that it is a decision-driven, smart, connected factory where all of the computer systems (hardware and software) in the factory (ERP, machine controls, robots, etc.) are interconnected through a cyber-physical system. As such, operators make key performance decisions through data and those decisions can be tackled based on actual metrics.

The predictions of Industry 4.0 run the gamut. Some believe robots will save our economy. We will reshore thousands of jobs. All the repetitive, dangerous, menial tasks humans never wanted to do will suddenly be gone through the salvation of robots. Yet, other predictions claim robots will eliminate hundreds of thousands of jobs, greatly reduce career options, and eliminate over 25% of current jobs through automation.[31] The hardest hit will be low-skill, low-wage individuals; but all of us will eventually be out of our current jobs.

So which path is it? In our conversations with manufacturing leaders, there is little doubt that regardless of the prediction, the technologies of Industry 4.0 are poised to be game changers for every company, supply chain, and industry.

Agriculture offers us a history lesson on the implications of technological advances. Our country is now a significant exporter of food. We help feed the world in so many ways: food production outputs, food safety technologies, transportation and logistics, and the transfer of production knowledge and know-how. In the 1870s, 50% of the US population was employed in agriculture. Today, it is less than 2%. With automation and science, productivity has advanced greatly through technologies in planters and combines, plant science, and so many other innovations. While the employment percentage declined drastically, output increased significantly. In fact, productivity has doubled since 1948, ensuring our critical role in feeding humanity. Imagine what a farmer of the 1870s would think of his craft today (they probably would love a tractor's touch screen, but find data analysis painful).

Manufacturing is clearly on a parallel path. In the 1970s, manufacturing employment hovered around 27% of the labor market, whereas today it is around 10%. Meanwhile, productivity has nearly doubled since 1950, and manufacturing output is at an all-time high. Yet, as with any economic progress, we face challenges and uncertainties.

Yes, new technologies will destroy jobs (this should come as no surprise–the motor car replaced the carriage; tractors, the horse and plow, and so forth). And, yes, these technologies will also create new jobs and strengthen the competitive position and security of many others. It's a time of momentous change and opportunity. Now is also the time of significant responsibility for leaders to embrace this future of manufacturing for our companies, employees, and their families. Because, if not us, then who? What country? What industry competitor?

US manufacturers embracing Industry 4.0 will be poised to overcome growth obstacles by developing a strategic technology adoption plan. This means being clear about the problems to solve and the opportunities to act on, and seeking out knowledge partners, public and private, that can help leverage Industry 4.0 concepts and incorporate new technologies.

Here are the ten pillars of Industry 4.0. These pillars have the potential to change the game for Illinois manufacturers and inspire growth.

1. **Big data analytics.** Big data is massive amounts of unused data in the manufacturing industry which can be collected and analyzed. Companies are collecting data on a large scale, but no one has the format or structure to analyze the information. In fact, IMEC has helped clients structure, organize, and analyze data in Enterprise Resource Planning System (ERP), Material Resource Planning (MRP),

Customer Resource Management, and Resource Management. These analytics are happening in real-time, so our clients are poised to make quick changes depending on market trends. In the words of data scientist W. Edwards Deming: "Without data, you're just another person with an opinion."

2. **Autonomous robots.** Autonomous robots are intelligent machines capable of executing tasks that are assigned to them without any human involvement. They play a huge part in the manufacturing industry to solve complex or unwanted tasks that cannot be solved by humans. The impacts autonomous robots create for manufacturers are providing mobility, functionality, cost-saving, and dexterity. Examples include welding, material handling, picking, packing, cutting, gluing, and painting, among others.
3. **Simulation.** A simulation is a helpful tool that helps manufacturers create virtual representations of a part or process on a digital platform. The digital tools help allow for planning and capacity analysis without having to represent equipment. The power of simulations is to run a full-scale process, operation, and design without needing to incur the full expense upfront. It provides a digital format for teams to discuss options and recognize challenges to make a better decision.
4. **Horizontal and vertical system integration.** For horizontal system integration, companies often develop a competitive approach to business. In the

past, this meant when an organization's facilities merged internally, the approach was often single-sided. One facility and one approach would surface. However, in horizontal integration, and the advent of big data analytics, an organization can adopt the best practices from both entities. This approach is consistent with the mergers of outside competitors or other companies. Most companies do not have a method to adopt or handle another company's big data. The horizontal integration will require extensive knowledge and transparency of data and supporting algorithms in order to be successful in the integration.

For vertical systems, the integration of operational technology and information technology across the enterprise form a seamless data exchange, with potential analysis and decision making. Vertical integration breaks down the barriers between functional units with the company to share data. Incorporation of big data analytics will provide for a starting point on what to share and how to share.

5. **The Industrial Internet of things (IIoT).** Industrial Internet of Things consists of smart devices that bridge the communication gap between machines and humans. These smart devices enable processors, sensors, and communication hardware to collect data from its respected environment. The benefits of smart IIoT devices are providing a real-time look into how the company's system

and processes work, so it can deliver insights into its operations and transparency into customer transactions. A prime example of IIoT devices is "interconnected sensors, instruments, and other devices networked together with computers' industrial applications."[32]

6. **Cloud computing.** Cloud computing brings various advantages to multiple data sets involved in smart manufacturing. With the use of the cloud, the range of data sharing increases exponentially through cloud storage. Clients do not have to deal with the upkeep of the software, including technical support, hardware/software maintenance, and security. This is great news for small to midsize manufacturers without an extensive information technology group. The core functionality of cloud computing is to store captured data that can be accessed from any location for further analysis.
7. **Additive manufacturing**. Additive manufacturing or 3D printing refers to producing customized goods as per an individual customer's orders. It uses a three-dimensional digital model to tell a machine to add or print material at a specific location. The most common way is the "prototype method" which helps produce small batches by gaining advantages of having less stock on their hand and overproduction. This reduces the cost and time inefficiencies for the manufacturer and provides more value for the end-user.

8. **Augmented Reality.** Augmented Reality is a tool that deploys virtual images over real-world objects with the help of our IoT devices or virtual glasses. Currently, end-user tasks like maintenance applications and training occur through audio or video application. Augmented Reality technology can help enhance this human-machine interaction and give the end-user remote control access on maintenance tasks virtually in real-time. Therefore, safety, efficiency, or effectiveness can be detected, reducing human error.
9. **HR technology**. Using technology to survey employees and gain insightful information allows organizations to make workforce and cultural improvements, resulting in engaged employees and increased retention rate. Other benefits increased performance, motivated employees, and reduced turnover. Some HR technology aids in hiring and recruiting, online learning, and individual wellness tracking.
10. **Cybersecurity.** While we will be addressing this more in the next section, cybersecurity is a must-have tech requirement. Its destructive impact on the business environment is undeniable. Actively identify, process, and act on data to improve the effectiveness of your organization. Cybersecurity calls for protecting your assets, data, and information from damaging the organization either by loss of market share, loss of new products, data breaches, or other risks to intellectual property.

MITIGATING CYBER RISK IN A VIRTUAL WORLD

Every organization has some level of risk that impacts the organization. Regardless of whether you have a formal quality management system or must meet regimented regulations, identify and plan for all potential risks to your organization. The National Institute of Standards and Technology (NIST) has created a guide for conducting risk assessments.

Consideration of technology solutions as well as good business practice solutions will form a top tier risk mitigation strategy. The immediate challenge top of mind: "How can I protect my digital assets from a cyber-attack?" Key vulnerabilities to a cyberattack are information technology/ operational technology (IT/OT), infrastructure, digital information, and Internet of Things (IoT) devices. Here are points to consider:

IT/OT infrastructure concerns. An immediate risk to any organization is its IT/OT infrastructure. Additionally, 43% of the cyber-attack targets were small to midsize businesses.[33] This happens, in great part, due to a system not having the capacity to support the increase in information flow (when the system is being overwhelmed), giving hackers an opportunity to strike.

To mitigate this risk, NIST has developed NISTIR 8183 Cybersecurity Framework Manufacturing Profile. This document provides cybersecurity framework (CSF) implementation details developed for the manufacturing environment. The framework is used by many manufacturers as a roadmap for reducing cybersecurity risk as it aligns with manufacturing sector goals and industry best practices. The manufacturing framework is meant to enhance but not to replace current cybersecurity standards and industry guidelines that the manufacturer is embracing.

IT security concerns. As remote work has increased, so have the challenges of internal networking and cybersecurity challenges. To make matters worse, some organizations have multiple IoT devices, which increase the risk of getting hacked–the attack surface is greater with more devices connected and communicating.

With these cybersecurity concerns, a few elementary cybersecurity considerations might be:

- Is the Wi-Fi connection secure?
- Are all IoT devices updated with the appropriate updates, anti-virus, firewall, and security tools?
- If you are a small business owner, how well is your information protected?
- Do all employees receive adequate instruction regarding system security policies and procedures?

To tackle these challenges for small business owners, NIST has developed an interagency report: NISTIR 7621 Rev.1 Small Business Information Security: The Fundamentals, as a guideline regarding cybersecurity for small business and presented in non-technical language.

Also, if your organization is using multiple IoT devices then follow the guidelines of NISTIR 8228 Consideration for

Managing Internet of Things (IoT) Cybersecurity and Privacy Risks. This guideline helps organizations better understand and manage the cybersecurity and privacy risks associated with their individual IoT devices throughout their life cycles.

Technology: virtual reality (VR). Occupational Safety and Health Administration (OSHA), the military, finance, and sociology have classically used a series of profile questionnaires prior to, and after, any risk-taking event. The bias associated with the classic questionnaire approach can lead to a general under-representation of preparedness when facing the risk-taking event. However, through the use of virtual reality, a series of scenarios may be presented to the trainee, allowing for a more realistic response during risk-taking events.

Technology: digital twin. Creation of a model that provides digital feedback of an entity provides an opportunity to evaluate a system through simulation. The digital twin can be used to simulate risk in the virtual world through test and evaluation. The military standard MIL-E-7016F provides an example of evaluation of AC and DC bus load current on the electrical systems in aircraft. The digital twin will simulate a load and demonstrate the effects of the connections of all essential systems to minimize the load on the electrical system. This method allows for testing in development prior to any financial outlay of raw materials, testing in manufacturing, and product improvement or risk reduction of higher risk systems.

Technology: Augmented Reality (AR). The Cosumnes Services District Fire Department (CSDFD) Augmented Reality Emergency Response System is a series of SMART tools and methods to allow first responders to become immersed in situations that allow the participant the opportunity to evaluate an emergency situation and respond. As this is a training method, the augmented reality tracks positioning and activity.

However, augmented reality allows for customization in developing risk mitigation strategy for high-risk concerns before an emergency. Chemical facilities, manufacturing facilities, or even service industries are best suited with actual simulated events to make errors before they count.

Processes: risk consideration in system. Technology provides significant advantages in doing more with less. However, in creating more value, the tools and systems earmarked for the improvement may generate a potential risk. Consider the Internet of Things (IoT) devices. These tools provide the ability to connect dissimilar devices and tools to a vast infrastructure of computer networks, shared databases, and basic signaling between them. However, the risk associated with specifying, purchasing, and installing these devices can create a risk. Baseline specifications should consider security protocols or consider baseline testing of IoT devices as part of the product development. Sources used to test devices should consider the Open Web Application Security Project that evaluates the top ten vulnerabilities of the IoT architecture.

INDUSTRY 4.0 CAN SOLVE PRODUCTIVITY GAPS: FIVE ACTIONS FOR LEADERS OF SMALL AND MIDSIZE MANUFACTURING COMPANIES

While we remain one of the most productive nations, manufacturing productivity has proved flat in recent decades. Productivity and output per hour is a vital foundation for stronger companies, higher wages, and rising standards of living.

Dig deeper and we find a significant productivity gap between large and small manufacturers. Larger manufacturers have approximately 60% higher productivity per employee than smaller manufacturers. Contrast this to 1967 when productivity per employee was "only" 26% higher in larger companies. Small and midsize manufacturers are 99% of manufacturing establishments and 60% of supply chain costs. Their productivity is essential for our nation's industrial strength.

Industry 4.0 technologies help solve productivity challenges. Many of these technologies hold the promise of step-function productivity improvements at reasonable prices for the small and midsize manufacturer. Yet, small manufacturers are lagging in new technology adoption relative to their larger counterparts.

The good news is there is a path forward. There are solutions. (After all, manufacturing leaders are a thoughtful and entrepreneurial group.)

Start with the problem. Get clear on the likely root causes. Where are the biggest productivity improvement opportunities in your business? Write each one down using a sentence or two. Continuous improvement approaches like lean and quality provide a path. Your unwavering commitment to a continuous improvement culture will give you ample insights into productivity improvements.

Lay out the options. It's fun to think about new technologies that can solve our greatest woes. Identify all the ways to solve a problem. The answer is likely multiple solutions. Don't be surprised if part of the solution can come from "simple" things, such as training or modest design improvements.

Scout technologies that create big improvement. There are plenty of cool tools out there, such as robotics, 3D printing, safety and ergonomic monitoring systems, and more. Look for panel discussions hosted by manufacturing associations throughout Illinois, research options online, and talk to other manufacturers on what they use and why. Sharing best practices is one of the best ways to research technology.

Explore your cyber risks. Prepare, implement new practices, and be vigilant. Cybersecurity is a practice to "own" within your company. Look for board members or advisors who have cybersecurity experience.

Develop skills for the workforce. This is perhaps the hardest of all. The future of work is already here. Yet, we know we still need to develop the basic skills in problem-solving and continuous improvement. We need to figure out the relevant skills for our future needs. We need to capture the legacy knowledge of retirees. And, we have a societal responsibility to upskill the individuals who may be left behind as technology replaces work they would have otherwise done.

HOW TO STRUCTURE LARGE DATA SETS

Large data sets are useful in manufacturing for many reasons: predictive analytics, reducing waste, managing supply chain risk, and inventory management, among others. When analyzing large data sets or "big data," there are basic analytical steps that pave the way for more strategic decision-making.

Pooling data from a valid source. Finding a valid source of data is a key factor in having a strategic and structured response to crisis. In response to this, major enterprises with extensive and robust digital platforms are collaborating with new "open data" platforms designed to promote big data sharing during the crisis like Google Cloud, AWS, and Microsoft Azure. These platforms are able to capture a real-time view of a situation by leveraging large, publicly available data sets. For example, relative to the pandemic, data includes local shelter-in-place policies, various health reporting, transit resources, and mobility patterns to show how public behaviors are impacting the spread of the virus.

Big data interoperability framework. After pooling the right data sets, crafting an agile response can be time consuming, especially during a crisis. Certain businesses might have the resources for suitable data analytics to create that quick impact, but others may not. To assist, the National Institute of Standards and Technology (NIST) has developed a Big Data Interoperability Framework (NBDIF). This framework includes big data taxonomies, use cases, data security and privacy, among other attributes.

This framework helps when you are analyzing large data sets using any computing platform so that data can be moved from one platform to another. It also provides an option for scaling up digital information from small desktop setups to a larger environment with many processor nodes, providing time-critical data, and promoting informational insights. If your organization is new to big data analytics, the nine-volume framework can be a useful guide.

Large data sets can be overwhelming, but a valuable commodity. Collecting, storing, and analyzing big data leads the way to realizing impactful results.

DATA OVERLOAD

Performance data can be intimidating. The trendlines, data, charts, and information you have access to is akin to gold, but you're afraid to touch it in the event you're off on your calculations or interpretation. This should be easy, you tell yourself. Except it isn't. So, you grab a couple more cookies and continue to self-coach: *Just examine it, show some good bar graphs, dig into some of the details, then make good decisions. I can see information about what staff are doing, which clients we are working with, and our financial situation on a daily, weekly, and monthly basis. I should be able to know exactly what is happening, where we are being successful, who is struggling, and where and how to take action.*

Yet, it really isn't that simple at all. Here's the dilemma: when you are only looking at the data, you are only looking at the trees. To make sense of it all, you have to see the lush, green forest.

We all have an incredible amount of data at our fingertips. The amount will only increase as we continue to invest in sensors, automation, and data connections, but it is not easy to interpret. It can also be hard to pull out the actions that are needed to make improvements. Some data we may never need. Yet we seem to have this insatiable urge to know everything about everything. So, what does it mean to see the forest? It means understanding what you are trying to do with the data so you can turn it into a picture with which you take action. Think about it as though you are looking at a picture on your phone. You don't look at every individual pixel, you put all those pixels together to make a picture.

Again, we return to basics–the basics of problem-solving. We've explored this in previous sections; but, honestly, can we ever cover the topic too much (if you're nodding your head "yes," stay with us). Whether it's data or an engineering design for a new part, defining the problem is step one.

To understand the data, we need to look at it within the right context. What are the answers the data needs to hand over? Create a problem statement: in the opening example, the problem was guiding performance at an individual, team, or enterprise level. Where do you go from there? How about building a dashboard that makes corrections so you're heading in the right direction? To decide on the best dashboard, think through what decisions are needed to make short-term course corrections and what alerts will sound to know there was real trouble ahead. Once those decisions are identified, you can define the key data to keep you and the rest of the team on track.

Sometimes you will need to see an individual tree. However, most of the time you will want to venture further through the forest, traveling faster and unencumbered.

THE BIG PLAY: DIGITAL TRANSFORMATION

A Conversation with Craig Van den Avont, President GAM Enterprises in Mount Prospect, IL

Craig Van den Avont is the President of GAM Enterprises, a manufacturer of precision mechanical drive solutions used in motion control and automation technology. Naturally, his company isn't afraid of embracing new technology.

If you were to walk into GAM Enterprises' factory, you would notice that all departments are well-equipped with technology, not solely the engineering department. This is because GAM uses technology, not just to make its products better, but also to streamline processes and improve workflow.

Technology is not, however, foolproof. When the company applied its ERP system to a simple, manual process, the outcome was too complicated, and the manual process was put back into play. Too much data is also a potential problem. Someone has to manage, review, and create reports based on the information. Just because you can collect data, doesn't mean it is all equally important. When trying to use data to improve your business, Van den Avont advises selecting only the important metrics to measure and review.

Van den Avont joined IMEC virtually to discuss how digital technology has transformed his company.

IMEC: How has your company transformed digitally in the last few years, and how can you incorporate technology more?

CV: We've done a lot of work automating the design process and then automating workflow. We looked at the front office, and then also the factory.

IMEC: What was the biggest thing you have done with technology that has saved GAM Enterprises both time and money?

CV: Every order had to go to our design engineering department, and they would have to design certain components or certain features of the product for every single product that went out the door. [He points out:]

[The Problem:] All products were custom ordered, so how can you use automation to cut down on design time?

[The Idea:] Even though the component is custom, we could standardize the steps in the design process. Once the design process was standardized, we could automate it.

[The Solution:] Automated the whole custom-design functionality with artificial intelligence (AI).

Our orders are custom, so we couldn't install a machine that would create the exact same product over and over again. With the use of AI though, we were able to cut down on the work the design team had to go through to get an order ready for production.

IMEC: Prior to the adoption of AI, a GAM engineer would have to pull up all the drawings and the information to design each individual component. While each component of the products is unique, you installed software in place that can standardize the design process. What's the impact of this?

CV: We took what used to take forty-five minutes to an hour and got it down to about seven minutes. Once a product model is done, we automated the process for sending that model to the engineer.

IMEC: How did you know the expense and time upfront would be worth it?

CV: You just know if you can cut your design time from forty-five minutes to an hour down to seven minutes, you don't need to run the math to know there's a payback on this and it really makes sense.

IMEC: What was the hardest part?

CV: The hardest part is just taking the time to get it done. There is, unfortunately, no way around the time a company has to put in upfront to automate their workflow, but they will reap the benefits every day.

IMEC: How do you make digital transformation part of your work culture?

CV: You have to prioritize your strategic initiatives. If your strategic objective is to integrate a new machine or break into a new market, you have to make time in your company's already busy schedule to work on that goal. One way to lessen the load is to delegate and assign those projects to project champions and make digital transformation a part of everyone's job for that year.

[Relative to GAM's other front office digital transformation, it's] done a lot to improve efficiencies, streamline processes, and make GAM more profitable.

[Relative to GAM's other shop floor digital transformations, it's] cut down time for people transferring parts from machine A to machine B. This is now a "one and done" step, where once the employee loads up a machine, they don't have to touch that part again until there is a finished product ready.

IMEC: You mentioned that GAM Enterprises would rather pay people to program those machines and set up those machines rather than transfer parts, because setting up the machines requires a higher level of skill. Why was that digital transformation important?

CV: We like to spend our money on our employees and make sure they are utilized to their fullest potential.

IMEC: Sometimes there is a fear of becoming too dependent on technology. Do you see that as a potential problem in your organization? Why or why not?

CV: It's a problem in any organization. Sometimes a manual process and the older way of doing things are just fine. Not everything has to be put through a computer system and automated.

You may use technology but keep it simple–simple to use, simple to understand, and don't make a simple process complicated.

IMEC: What has technology given your organization?

CV: Efficiency and information. Really, that's the biggest thing. Another part of digitization is data. We know how long an order sat in sales, and how long an order sat in engineering, and how long it sat in material planning before it is released to the floor. We have dashboards everywhere.

IMEC: What kind of data is on those screens?

CV: The dashboard in the sales department has sales metrics, the dashboard in the engineering department has engineering metrics, and the dashboard in the general office has financial data, data on what orders are shipping today, etc. This data is real-time as well, as there wouldn't be much use for old data. Some of the metrics are updated every couple of minutes, while others may update once or twice per day.

IMEC: Why is data monitoring important?

CV: You don't know what you don't know, but sometimes you dig into a piece of data and it starts leading you down a path, and it starts telling you something you didn't realize was even going on.

IMEC: Where will you go next?

CV: We're currently deploying cobots on the shop floor. Trying to figure out once we get better at using those cobots to increase their workday, how to expand that, use them more, etc.

[There is] so much we can do on the quality side. If we can use automated quality measuring systems and have that data fed back into the machines, [the machines could] automatically adjust.

IMEC: If you were to give advice to a manufacturer who hasn't integrated technology into their organization, what is the simplest way for them to start?

CV: The best way to start is to really understand what your machines are doing.

IMEC: What do you mean by that?

CV: Get some software to monitor the machines and what they're doing–and not just what you think they're doing. This could mean measuring how long it takes your machine to make a part, or how often your machines sit idle.

Start with just a couple of top-level metrics and pick one or two leading indicators that you think drive those top-level metrics and measure the indicators. Then, drive actions that will improve the leading indicators.

FILE THIS UNDER DIGITAL TRANSFORMATION

One way GAM uses data is to monitor machines. This includes analyzing machine performance, what the machines are really doing, and if they are operating at full capacity.

In the front office, GAM uses data as a means to monitor orders as they go through the system. "We have data everywhere," Van den Avont said, and he was not kidding. Accounting, sales, and the shop floor all have large airport-style dashboard screens. If something falls outside a normal parameter, not only can GAM's dashboards display that, but the company has automated their system to send out a notification email to the right department warning them of this error.

GAM Enterprises hopes to push their automated design process back even further, into customers' hands. In the future, a customer may be able to custom-configure their product themselves online. This configuration would then flow directly into GAM's ERP system where products would then automatically begin being made.

Chapter 7

COMPETING DURING CRISIS: RESPOND, RECOVER, REBOUND

You can.

At times, events occur that test our vulnerabilities. You can point to these throughout history: The Great Depression, Y2K, Hurricane Katrina, 9/11, the Great Global Recession and, most recently, the pandemic. In each instance, system shortcomings were exposed, jobs disappeared, and people's lives were changed. In manufacturing, crisis comes by way of any number of paths. Supply chain disruption, global economic fluctuations, lack of information to determine demand, workforce challenges, and data compromises lead the list.

One thing is certain: small steps lead to big leaps, moving you forward. Here are some basic questions we discuss with manufacturers:

- In the face of crisis, does your organization have a risk plan to refer to?
- Do you regularly review and update it?
- Do you have designated people who own it?
- Would you describe your organization as proactive or reactive when crisis descends?

A good place to start is by taking stock of your situation–long before you are in the middle of a crisis. Here's why: A crisis can severely affect how we aggregate and process information into a format we can use to operate effectively. Key people who might have the information may be shifted to other jobs or "all hands on deck" thinking creates knee-jerk reactions to events as they unfold. In this position, organizations are forced to make operational decisions with different "types" of information that might be incomplete, anecdotal, untimely, or inaccurate.

At IMEC, we spend quite a bit of time looking at information flows and related tools and methods to provide a baseline understanding of any "new" event. The efforts inspire a new awareness for how to embolden an organization in a time of crisis.

By recognizing shortcomings early in the flow of information we use to operate in today's environment, we can capture and prioritize improvement opportunities to be implemented when we are back at full strength, whether it be next month, or next year.

The key is to take the time to document the challenges as they occur. Future improvements will be built by the information you gather today. Your greater, deeper awareness is a good companion to most of the topics covered in this chapter, from preparing your workforce, to assessing risk, to a crisis checklist.

On the following pages, prepare to armor up–so that your efforts now will help your manufacturing company better respond, recover, and rebound later.

IMPLEMENTING STANDARD WORK STRIVES FOR CONSISTENCY IN A CRISIS ENVIRONMENT

Standard work means determining and documenting the ideal process to produce correct and consistent results. It represents the best sequence and the most efficient methods to perform a process. In a crisis situation, consistency can become a coveted hallmark.

Standard work ensures that everything is done in a similar manner so that the work achieves the highest quality, best service, and lowest cost possible. In the world of lean manufacturing, this adherence to standard work has resulted in positive, repeatable results in a variety of industries. In fact, many believe that standard work should be one of the foundational tools to develop, implement, and maintain strategies to combat most crises in a lean manufacturing environment.

Standard work plays an important role in ensuring safety in a simple or complex manufacturing operation. Lean organizations rely on standard work in order to allow just-in-time production and delivery, and to create a baseline from which they can improve. Where there are no standards, there can be no improvement. Each time a standard is improved, it becomes the basis for future improvements. In new crisis situations, as evidenced by the pandemic, few standards exist in how to prepare and maintain a safe workplace and environment.

Benefits of standard work. Standard work is an important part of any sustainable improvement effort. Successful solutions must be standardized in order to remain effective over the long term. Many times, we come to a situation where a closed project needs to be reopened. This indicates that the problem was not effectively dealt with or there were no actions taken to sustain the gains. Using the pandemic as an example, if cleanliness and sanitation were not effectively dealt with, lives were put at risk.

The approach to initially prepare the workplace for a crisis sets the stage for exciting, new work procedures resulting in safer, more efficient, and more productive work areas. With increased repetition and consistent steps, quality will occur in a reliable and predictable manner. Individuality may be a good thing, but not when it comes to managing processes, as this may cause inconsistent results and lead to customer dissatisfaction. By ensuring that the work area is prepped the same way, employees will be more confident that they are working in a safe environment. This leads to improved productivity, decreased lead time, and reduced errors and wastes.

Standard work provides a method to document the process information in a written format. It is also considered a very useful learning tool. Newcomers and workers on the job use it to do their work more efficiently. Sharing this information creates a safer working environment, clarifies roles, and promotes problem-solving and teamwork. It is also an approach to document and share best practices at both local and global levels.

Standard operating procedures. Standard work can be embedded in the company's operation by using standard operating procedures (SOPs). While we cover this more in detail in the next section, let's define it here. An SOP is a document that describes the best way to execute a process and its activities to maintain consistent working practices. It represents what will be done, how it will be done, and who will be responsible for making sure it gets done.

Developing and implementing SOPs enables standard work to be effective and helps communicate it to those working in the process. SOPs are often used to document the project solution in order to sustain improvements that have been made.

Standard work and SOP documents may contain written instructions, drawings, flowcharts, photographs, checklists, or any other information needed to clearly communicate the standard. They usually include:

- The description and scope of the work
- Why things are done in a certain way
- The exact work sequence involved in which activities are completed

- The optimal amount of time needed for each activity
- The rate at which products must be produced to meet customer demand
- Responsibilities and work distribution
- Key points related to safety, quality, and performance
- The materials, equipment, and tools needed to complete the work
- A revision control system

Standard work documents should be created by consensus of those who actually do that work. People support what they help to create. These documents should be posted where the work is being done. This helps employees remember the proper activity sequence and ensure workplace standards are consistent. Visuals are used to demonstrate difficult concepts and reinforce the standard work. Use design and colors branded to your company's brand guidelines.

HOW TO DEVELOP AND IMPLEMENT A STANDARD OPERATING PROCEDURE

The following steps can serve as a guide to developing and implementing a standard operating procedure (SOP):

- With your team, clearly describe the purpose for writing the SOP (examples might include initial preparation of the work area; sanitizing before, during, and after the production run; and preparing and sustaining for the next period of operation)

- Understand the existing system for standard work
- Get permission to conduct Gemba Walks, where participants step out of their specific role, walk the plant floor, and talk to the people there
- Prepare existing documents (like checklists and flowcharts)
- Collect data, observe actual practices, interview people, and ask questions
- Analyze the current process and identify opportunities for improvement
- Write the SOP in a simple and visual way
- Test and review the draft SOP with the process performers, get input from them, and modify the SOP as necessary
- Approve the SOP, then post it in the workplace
- Train or retrain everyone as necessary to follow it
- Monitor for effectiveness and compliance

In the lean world, standard work is considered a foundational tool in developing and sustaining a safe environment and efficiently producing a quality product (sounds pretty good, right?). When properly implemented and maintained with vigor, standard work results in a safe and productive workplace.

A CHECKLIST: PRE-EMPLOYEE ENTRY

After developing standard operating procedures (SOPs), develop guidelines for employees returning to work post-crisis. Many of these points merit periodic review:

Safety:

- ☐ General infrastructure like lighting, restrooms,
- ☐ HVAC are working
- ☐ Emergency lighting is working
  All paths and emergency exits are clear
  All mandated employee training is up to date
- ☐ Check if new chemicals (disinfection/sanitation) have been introduced (if so, update your Hazcom program)
- ☐ Check for and dispose of expired materials
- ☐ Review necessary start-up procedures before turning machinery on
- ☐ Address employee concerns regarding safety, additional PPE, or other protective barriers

Network/Communication Systems:

- ☐ Facility network is working
- ☐ Timekeeping system is working
- ☐ ERP/CRM/inventory control systems are working
- ☐ Adequate inventories are available (PPE, raw materials, spare parts, etc)
- ☐ Wireless communications between workers, machines, and networks are working

Machine/Process Start-up:

Hydraulic Systems

- ☐ Check fluid levels
- ☐ Check for puddles/leaks
- ☐ Replace filters and fluids as necessary
- ☐ Check tube/hose condition
- ☐ Drain/clean reservoir
- ☐ Follow recommended start-up procedures, verify safety features are operational, and monitor unusual noises and vibrations
- ☐ Check for leaks after start-up

Electrical Cabinets

- ☐ Replace cabinet air filters
- ☐ Vacuum dust and dirt buildup
- ☐ Check for damaged components

Pneumatic Systems

- ☐ Drain water from tanks/lines
- ☐ Fill oilers
- ☐ Check compressor fluid levels
- ☐ Follow recommended start-up procedures, verify safety features are operational, and monitor to unusual noises and vibrations
- ☐ Listen for air leaks after start-up

Mechanical Systems

- ☐ Check gearbox fluid levels
- ☐ Check for stuck conveyor rollers
- ☐ Grease motors/bearings/chains
- ☐ Follow recommended startup procedures, verify safety features are operational, and monitor to unusual noises and vibrations

Chillers/Cooling Systems

- ☐ Check that airflow isn't blocked
- ☐ Check fluid levels
- ☐ Replace necessary filters
- ☐ Follow recommended startup procedures, verify safety features are operational, and monitor to unusual noises and vibrations

Material Handling Systems

- ☐ Complete all necessary checklists prior to use
- ☐ Visually inspect all equipment with a formal pre-use checklist
- ☐ Follow recommended startup procedures, verify safety features are operational, and monitor to unusual noises and vibrations

FOUR STRATEGIES TO ADJUST AND IMPROVE CASH FLOW DURING A CRISIS

There's a quote by William Arthur Ward that goes like this: "The pessimist complains about the wind; the optimist expects it to change; the realist adjusts the sails."[34]

Maintaining adequate cash flow is a major factor when operating a healthy business in times of growth and prosperity. During tough times, however, it takes on an amplified role. The fundamentals of collecting receivables, reducing expenses, and reducing inventory investment are all still in play, but these need to be closely examined in challenging economic times.

Increase sales within your top relationships. Use an 80/20 approach to identify your customers by four segments based on revenue and profitability. This exposes hard data on where to focus your efforts for the most impact (and sets the table for better results in the long term). For your top two segments, consider the following:

- Solidify and increase the contact and relationship building
- Ask for new business
- Look for ways to add value to those top relationships

Accelerate collection of receivables. Consider offering discount terms for prompt payment. While you receive less, you improve fluidity and options and reduce the risk of default. Also, avoid being a bank. You may find yourself where you cannot secure better terms from your suppliers yet might be extending more generous terms to your customers. If you choose to be a lender, get something for it such as committed long-term orders. Lastly, offer discounted terms strategically. Offers today may turn into unexpected commitments over time. Be clear that the offers are due to extraordinary circumstances, and ask for something of value in return.

Evaluate and adjust your inventory investment strategy. Don't necessarily slash inventory spending completely. Purchasing wisely would be a better course. If you can get reduced prices for your materials, it may be advantageous to build your inventory to ultimately reduce inputs per unit. However, in most cases, paying slightly more for reduced quantities and more frequent shipments may fit your short-term cash flow goals in a better fashion.

Use the moment to improve processes and profitability. Now is the time to evaluate, train, and retool. Improving quality in processes results in short term benefits of reduced cost, improved productivity, and increased profitability. It also can improve the employee experience, resulting in longer term outcomes of reduced turnover, increased retention of talented staff, and improved recruitment efforts.

STRATEGY IN A TIME OF UNCERTAINTY

Albert Einstein is quoted as saying, "In the midst of every crisis, lies great opportunity." If this is true, what is the opportunity for your organization when crisis hits? Where is your playbook (besides the one you are holding!)? How can you lead the organization to not only survive but thrive in the future?

We've mentioned the Baldrige Excellence Framework a few times so far because it enables companies to create and sustain organizational excellence. Even in crisis-management mode, we have found that this framework helps organizations. Here are specific ideas to put strategy into play.

Ensure organizational continuity. Can an organization ever be fully prepared for a disaster, emergency, or crisis? Different organizations are more susceptible to risks and disruptions of their operations. Effective business continuity planning considers prevention (where possible), seamless continuity of operations, and recovery. Consider your workforce, supply network, and clients. How we respond in a crisis allows us to reinforce our organizational culture inclusive of open communication, workforce health, and an engaged workforce. The framework asks us to identify changing engagement drivers–which can be both emotional and intellectual.

Let's take IMEC as a vivid example. While not perfect (we humbly admit), we established a definitive response to the COVID-19 crisis, including several initiatives aimed at employee engagement and open communications. Our leaders established meetings to explain and discuss developments. We held voluntary meetings for teams to discuss what was on their minds and the minds of clients.

Our president conducted open discussion calls with groups of employees to address concerns and share ideas. Family care packages included candy, gift cards for dinner delivery, and other items for employees.

To address client concerns, IMEC established a helpline to address questions and needs within one business day. Our website has been modified to connect suppliers with those in need of supplies based on COVID-19 items, including masks and ventilators. These actions have allowed our organizational culture of working together and serving others to be maintained while living our vision, mission, and values.

Look for strategic opportunities. Colleges and universities are also a good example of strategy during uncertain times. Across the country students were sent home, and courses shifted online in 2020. While in-person, undergraduate learning has long been the norm, online became a reliable alternative, and not a surprising one, as distance learning has gained speed over the last decade..

By going back to your strategy in the face of great challenge, you put your organization in a stronger position to compete. For colleges and universities, the crisis accelerated a trend which was already underway. It is highly unlikely that higher educational institutions will revert exclusively to their old model. Innovation, though, will likely transform future success.

Can you define a strategic opportunity? The Baldrige Framework asks us to consider when circumstances require a shift in our plans and then rapid execution of new plans.

How do you integrate the need for transformational change and organizational agility? What should you stop doing, start doing, or do differently going forward?

Recognize when the time is available to reconsider plans. What have you learned as an organization? Has the marketplace changed? Have customer needs and expectations changed? With our example of colleges and universities, students may expect and demand a more flexible learning environment moving forward. Identify your potential strategic opportunities and your ability to innovate.

A systems perspective sticks. How can we sustain improvements once we have reflected, adjusted, and implemented our new strategy? The framework helps us to identify and leverage our strengths and prepare to face our challenges. It guides us to address issues which are deemed important by an organization. However, it does not prescribe how you should structure your operations. These decisions are made by your organization by defining processes around leadership, strategy, customers, measurement, workforce, operations, and results.

Once an organization defines all components of their system, they can be managed to achieve the mission of your organization, its ongoing success, and performance excellence. This is called a systems perspective. Regular internal assessment helps improve the system moving forward so success sticks.

Many companies who are ISO registered are required to identify risks and opportunities, as well as develop a response plan and integrate the response into their quality management system. While this sounds good, it became inadequate during the onset of a crisis because ISO9001 asks a company to identify "what they will do if something happens." As of this writing, companies need a comprehensive plan to manage the business through a crisis already in play.

Here are ideas to help you respond more effectively:

- Emergency management leader
- Emergency management team (with defined roles)
- Team processes and procedures (including return to work policy)
- Communication plan (internal, external, and key contacts)
- Employee training
- Evacuation plan
- Property protection and security (facility shutdown, records preservation, and building information)
- Community outreach plan
- Recovery and restoration (supply chain, logistics, operations, human resources, and information systems)
- Implementation and maintenance (conduct drills, train employees, and an annual plan audit)

Continuity planning. As part of continuity planning, develop a comprehensive business impact plan and identify both short-term and long-term actions. The business impact plan should contain all of the elements identified above, with the emergency management leader serving as the owner of the document. Review and update at a frequency (daily, weekly, monthly) that ensures you are ready to respond, recover, and rebound.

FOUR KEY ELEMENTS OF AN EFFECTIVE RISK MANAGEMENT PROGRAM

Do you have a risk plan? If not, read on. We provide four key elements of an effective risk management program so that your organization can be more proactive with initial risk management plans, taking into consideration operations, procurement, processes, and personnel.

An effective risk management program combines the evaluation of risk with the deployment of resiliency. Risk is defined as the likelihood and consequence of events, at any point in the organization, to disrupt the normal flow of supplies and result in negative impacts to downstream channel product flow and supporting infrastructure and services. Resiliency is the capability of a company or network to recover quickly and cost-effectively from an event, with minimal or no impact to the normal flow of supplies to the organization. A risk management program has four key elements.

Risk identification. Risk identification can be a challenging first step as it can be difficult to identify the "unknown-unknowns." For example, the potential localized risk of fire, flood, or tornado at your facility is a very common and quantifiable risk. We can estimate the cost of a building, loss of inventory, and recovery time to resume operations. However, estimating the disruption in each segment of our supply chain that each of these more common events might cause makes the identification impact of risk more difficult. We only need to think back a few years to the tsunami which struck Japan to recall the many businesses and industries that were affected due to then-unknown lower tier suppliers who sustained damage or catastrophic loss when the wave hit.

Risk identification may also be a completely internal event such as the loss of a key team member with no backup capability or understudy. An ineffective or unresponsive process which leads to a poor response, or no response at all when an unplanned or unexpected event occurs is another simple example of an internal risk. An example might be a supplier's gradual increase in lead time over a period of time without suitable identification or alert to the organization.

Risk assessment. Quantifying the probability of an event to happen (occurrence) with its impact (severity) and our ability to have advance warning (trigger rating) is the foundation of an assessment of risk. These three measurements allow the creation of a risk index number, a mathematical way to quantify the impact of an event. The higher the risk index number (or risk priority number), the more severe of an impact an event will have on an organization and this number is also an indicator as to where actions should be taken to mitigate a risk.

After potential risks are identified and assessed, they are evaluated, and one or more techniques to manage or mitigate risks may be implemented:

- Avoidance (eliminate the risk or cease the activity)
- Reduction (reduce the likelihood or impact)
- Transfer (shift the risk to a third party skilled in handling the situation)
- Retention (accept the risk as is)

A key component of this assessment and mitigation step is the development of a recovery or action plan in the instance where a risk event has occurred. Ask as part of your management assessment: What will we do? How will we do it? Who is responsible for seeing that it's been done in a timely and correct manner?

Risk action management. Execution of the risk plan is the point where identification and assessment will begin to positively affect your organization. Risk action plans are developed and implemented. Risk mitigation plans for suppliers, vendors, personnel, and, yes, even customers, are put into place and validated. Trigger warnings, monitoring methods, and data is monitored to provide advance warning of a potential or impending risk event. Success of this step is to accept that this is a continually evolving and maturing process. Risks will come and go, their potential severity will increase and decrease, sometimes in a matter of days. The cost of mitigation for the risk will change. With each issue, the risk index number will change and a corresponding adjustment to the management of the risk plan and program will be required.

Risk reporting and monitoring. Identifying, assessing, quantifying, and managing risk will produce even better outcomes when there is access to timely, accurate, and actionable information. Daily, and sometimes hourly, updates may be necessary to effectively monitor the risk triggers. Trigger ratings are used to manage if specific events happen and drive a reaction to risk events. Regularly test scenarios to validate risk management plans and programs.

The deployment of a risk management program and the underlying risk management plans have become a necessary component of comprehensive business continuity and disaster recovery planning efforts. Make your risk management program part of your organization's strategic plan to be reviewed at least once a year. Monitoring and mitigation put you in a position to win, responding faster and more intelligently to risk events as they arise.

SHORT-TERM DISRUPTIONS FUEL LONG-TERM GROWTH PLANNING AND CONTINUOUS LEARNING

As we've seen from the many examples and through the eyes of history, the most important element of crisis is our ability to learn from it and even be inspired by it. Short-term disruption is uncomfortable, even painful, to endure. We wish to turn back the clock to more comfortable and uneventful times. However, life does not always work that way.

Oftentimes, that is a good thing.

Taking stock of what is being learned and applying it to a long-term growth strategy going forward is undeniably the rule of thumb for modern manufacturers to compete globally.

While it may cause us to reframe our growth strategy, it also gives us permission to reimagine the future.

Debrief After Disruption

A few important questions ahead of the strategy planning process should be:

- What did we learn?
- Where were we strong?
- Where could we improve?
- How has the marketplace changed?
- How well did we communicate with our customers?
- How well did we communicate with one another internally?
- Did we stay focused as a company on the same goals?
- Were there new or different types of customers we acquired?
- How nimble were we in meeting customer needs?
- How have our customer needs and their expectations of us changed?
- What is the new baseline for these expectations, and can we accommodate it?
- How are we stronger on the other side of disruption?
- In hindsight, how can we minimize the impact of future business disruptions?
- Armed with new knowledge and experience, what is our company's future state?
- Have we updated our risk assessment plan?

Answering these questions will help you plan for future growth. Think innovatively, learn along the way, diversify your base of customers, be flexible and nimble to anticipate opportunities, and make changes to stay ahead of the competition.

A CHECKLIST: 9 PRACTICAL MOVES MANUFACTURERS CAN MAKE TO RESPOND TO CRISIS

Use the following checklist to ready your team in the face of crisis and unexpected disruption.

Model Your Cash Flow Position

- ☐ Prioritize essential expenses and delay expenses considered discretionary.
- ☐ Bank lines of credit and small business loans may be appropriate to supplement available cash reserves.
- ☐ Explore alternative funding support.

Check Insurance Coverage

- ☐ Consult with your attorney to confirm what your obligations are under the latest Family and Medical Leave Act (FMLA) updates.
- ☐ Consult with your insurance agent to confirm what your obligations are under the latest FMLA updates.

Communicate with Your Customers

- ☐ Reach out directly to customers and communicate clearly and consistently. Make sure they know you are open for business. Encourage their feedback on how you can make it easier for them to purchase your products and services. This will go a long way to solidifying your relationship with them.
- ☐ Use your social media presence to keep customers updated. If you typically don't use social media, now is the perfect time to investigate how to leverage all the available platforms and create an online presence, making it easier for you to connect with customers.

Prepare Your Employees for the Future State

- ☐ Clearly communicate with your employees that they will be protected to the best of your ability. It goes without saying that you want to retain key people who drive your business. Keep communication going on a consistent basis until things return to normal.
- ☐ If layoffs are unavoidable, be honest with employees and explore all you can do to support them.
- ☐ Consider conducting weekly team huddles to keep all employees informed as to changing priorities and what will be expected of them until things return to normal.
- ☐ Be clear with employees about business policies and safety protocols relative to a specific crisis.

Update Your Cybersecurity Framework

- ☐ There is a criminal element that will use a crisis to exploit vulnerable company computer fire wall defenses. Update your defenses against data breaches, phishing, and other villainous threats common when vulnerabilities run high.

Support Your Remote Workers

- ☐ Working remotely may not be an ideal option, however company leaders need to assess what functions can be done remotely and what must be completed in the office. This may depend on job function, employee skill, and family situation at home for the employee.
- ☐ Maximize the effectiveness of your organization's internal communications by leveraging technology for virtual meetings (Zoom, WebEx, Skype, or Microsoft Teams), focused and productive conversations and knowledge sharing outside of email (Slack), and workflow management (Trello, Basecamp, or Jira).

Consider Shifting Your Strategic Priorities

- ☐ In the face of crisis, your strategic plan most likely will need to be revisited and modified. Priorities will need to be adjusted with greater emphasis on essential product support.

- ☐ If you don't have a strategic plan, now is the perfect time to develop one to guide your efforts through a challenging business climate.

Manage What's in Your Control

- ☐ Categorize issues and delegate resources around:
  - Urgent and mission critical
  - Important but not urgent
  - Nice to have but not important nor urgent
- ☐ Be realistic: achieve one thing each day rather than trying to address a number of items all at once.
- ☐ Identify your assets and apply the best resources to address a task or issue.

Plan for What's Next

- ☐ Use this time to develop plans for greater effectiveness and efficiency in your workflow, especially on your production lines as demand begins to regenerate.
- ☐ Conduct critical maintenance and repairs on equipment to maximize output capacity as business conditions normalize.
- ☐ Prepare and cross-train team members to compensate for any attrition in your workforce.
- ☐ Design new products or extensions to your current product mix that can ramp up quickly, capitalizing on new revenue opportunities.

THE BIG PLAY: CONTINUOUS LEARNING

A Conversation with Jean Pitzo, CEO
Ace Metal Crafts in Bensenville, IL

Ace Metal Crafts is a manufacturer located just outside of Chicago. Ace is made up of 150 employees, many of whom relocated from countries outside the US in order to work for Ace. With so many ethnic cultures collaborating on one shop floor, Ace's CEO Jean Pitzo has seen more than her fair share of workplace crises. This interview is on how Ace was able to "respond, recover, and rebound" from just a few specific crises their workforce has faced.

CRISIS #1: WORKFORCE GAPS AND HIRING

IMEC: How does Ace Metal Crafts deal with the current talent gap in manufacturing?

JP: Our lack of being able to hire talent has kept us the size we are for many years. It is so hard for us to find a welder. Welding and CNC machinists are in incredibly high demand, and there's very low supply. We use agencies, we recruit online . . . We recruit any way we can think of. In the 80s, for some reason, they shut down all the tech schools, like the welding schools. In other countries, they didn't do that.

IMEC: How has that affected the hiring pool in America?

JP: Some of the talent that we need to hire is in Mexico or Europe or Bosnia, Croatia, or Vietnam. The baby boomer generation that knows how to make stuff is retiring, and then there's this big gap.

IMEC: What is your most reliable method for finding employees?

JP: When Ace does hire, the candidates usually don't come from online platforms or hiring agencies. Most actually come from employee referrals. Our employees bring in their family members, or they bring in people they know or who they worked with at another company.

Not only is this our most successful recruiting tool, but it is also the most cost efficient. When we bring in someone from an agency, we have to pay that agency $25,000 to $40,000, which is a lot more than the bonus we provide to employees for referring a new hire.

IMEC: How do you encourage employees to refer candidates?

JP: We pay them for every recruit that they bring in who stays for six months or longer. While at some companies this may lead to a lack of diversity, it increases our diversity since we already have a diverse team.

Even with the success of our referral program, we do still struggle to fill open positions at times.

IMEC: Out of your 150 or so employees, about ten are women. What do you do to increase women on your team?

JP: We try to get young girls interested in manufacturing. Every year, we partner with Triton College's Gadget Girls program. During this program, the Gadget Girls are able to participate in designing and fabricating a part, which our manufacturers then create before their eyes.

IMEC: Given the various languages spoken by your team, how do you communicate in routine meetings?

JP: When we meet, we speak in English, we put the slide up in English, and then we put the slide up in Spanish, and we say it in Spanish. Then we put the slide up in Polish and say it in Polish.

It's tedious and laborious. Every meeting is three times as long, but it's so worth it! If we gave our meetings only in English, 60-70% of our staff wouldn't receive the message at all. That would be a waste. You have to commit. You're either going to have three or four meetings in these different languages or you're going to have one meeting and make the entire staff sit there for the few minutes that it takes for the interpreter to say it in the other languages. And we do both; we mix it up.

IMEC: Overall, you are a very diverse organization. What are some misconceptions you have seen regarding diversity?

JP: I think diversity is a trigger word for people . . . I think that a lot of leaders in companies say 'Forget it, if they don't speak English, forget it! That's their problem.' That affects the culture in a negative way. The company pays the price of that attitude.

IMEC: Why do you believe that?

JP: You're going to miss some super-talented, great people.

IMEC: How can a company in a small town expand their hiring pool?

JP: You'll have to recruit in areas outside of your geographic location and pull them in and move them.

CRISIS #2: COMPETING CULTURES AND COLLABORATION

IMEC: How would you define ethnic "culture"?

JP: The food, the way you talk, what certain things and words mean to certain people, comes into play.

IMEC: Has Ace ever faced any employee clashes over cultural differences?

JP: In my earlier years, there would be some ethnic-type clashes or separation. We have Serbians and Bosnians that were in a war against each other in the 90s and now they work in our plant together and are great friends.

IMEC: How did you get these different cultures to work well together and see eye-to-eye?

JP: It's evolved over the years, but the biggest impact and the biggest thing we did–and we spent probably eight months to a whole year doing this–we decided what our values were. We put the values on a board and asked staff 'What does trust mean to you? How do you behave with trust?'

IMEC: Were there any surprising behaviors among your employees?

JP: One of the behaviors that is super important to most of the guys on the shop floor is 'I return what I borrow.' This behavior was very surprising to me. I would've never thought of this myself. I can't remember the last time I borrowed anything. Our employees have their own toolboxes and tools, which are sometimes lent out. Before these value meetings, the borrowing of tools on the shop floor led to accusations of stealing because not everyone was returning what they borrowed.

Behaving with respect was so different for people depending on how they grew up. We have one specific employee who grew up among gangs in Chicago's South Side. He was very young when he first started working at Ace, and when he was discussing what respect meant to him, he explained that if you disrespected him, he had to kill you. [This showed that respect can be a trigger word].

IMEC: It seems like there were definitely some strong opinions from your staff. What was the end result of these meetings?

JP: At the end of the eight months of discussing values and behaviors with employees, these meetings helped employees as a group understand what Ace values meant to them and how they can show those values in a work setting. For example, some ways we decided as a group to show respect at Ace were to return what you borrow, share your knowledge, keep your area neat and clean, and other similar behaviors.

IMEC: Did any other definitions or values surprise you?

JP: We wrote the word care out in English, but then again in Vietnamese, Bosnian, Serbian, Polish, and Spanish. The Spanish-speaking team actually spent fifteen minutes of that meeting trying to decide which word translated into the English word 'care.' In the end, they chose 'amor,' which actually means love, to represent care in Spanish. This was heartwarming.

IMEC: What about employee socialization? Is that difficult with so many different languages?

JP: I noticed that our employees were sticking with their ethnic group during lunch.

IMEC: What did you do about that?

JP: I asked one of our employees about it, and he explained it. I learned this the hard way. I don't think in English and [then have to] say it in a different language. It can be exhausting. It's such a relief for thirty minutes at lunch to not have to try to 'do the language thing.'

I accepted what is and didn't fight the fight anymore. While cultural harmony is important, I learned that lunchtime collaboration was a fight not worth fighting for.

CRISIS #3: TIME CONSTRAINTS AND CONTINUOUS LEARNING

IMEC: How does emotional intelligence courses benefit Ace and its employees?

JP: This course gets them to collaborate together. Topics include awareness, triggers, blame, shame, victimhood, and forgiveness. Forgiveness is my favorite course to teach. This enables employees on a shop floor to quickly forgive when something goes wrong and to move on to finding a solution. Because we teach so many people forgiveness, the speed of resolution is accelerated. Blame slows us down.

IMEC: Where did you acquire these courses?

JP: I wrote them, with the help of Deb Benning, VP of HR. We also have book clubs, which have been very successful.

IMEC: How are Ace book clubs structured?

JP: Participants are reading chapter one, and they highlight what they like in that chapter. One week or two weeks later, we will meet to review everyone's highlights and discuss the chapter.

IMEC: How do you get your shop floor to participate?

JP: Some people are very uncomfortable reading English in front of other people. In this case, I will offer to read that employee's highlights for them.

IMEC: Are these book clubs held during the lunch hour then?

JP: No, we don't do it during lunch. We pull them off the shop floor and lose productivity. That's how important it is to me.

IMEC: How else has Ace book clubs and emotional intelligence courses helped your employees?

JP: These initiatives don't just help employees' emotional intelligence while they are at work. One employee confided in me that he had full custody of his three children and that hitting his children was part of his discipline method. That was how this employee grew up himself, and instead of judging him, I realized the employee just wasn't aware of other disciplining methods. And I have to tell you, it takes a moment not to judge that.

A key factor in this was trust, because the employee trusted me enough to believe me that there was another way to raise his children. At the time, a lot of employees were raising young children, so one group decided to read and discuss a parenting book on discipline. This completely changed how that employee raised his children. Now his oldest is in college, his youngest is thirteen, and all three children are doing incredibly well. We have a ton of unbelievable stories like that, and he has thanked me a million times.

Teaching someone how to discipline their children, who thinks you're going to be in that sphere in a work environment?

CRISIS #4: SHIFTING PRIORITIES AND LEADERSHIP TRAINING

IMEC: Do you offer continuous learning for your leadership team as well?

JP: The biggest emphasis is with the leaders. The leaders need to be self-aware and confident of what their own triggers are to be great leaders.

IMEC: Why are triggers so important?

JP: People trigger you. Their behaviors trigger you and their answers trigger you or whatever they're complaining about today will trigger you, but the leader has got to rise above all of that to really hear the information being communicated.

Leaders can be brutally abusive. Leaders can be horrible, horrible people because they get triggered, they play favorites, etc. . . . We don't allow our leaders to be like that, period.

IMEC: Do you have an example of a type of leadership style you don't allow at Ace?

JP: I call them 'Gotcha Leaders'–this is a leader who leads with fear and is constantly looking for ways their employees messed up.

I could walk in my shop and find 500 things that are wrong, that is so easy, but walking in my shop and complimenting 500 times . . . that takes energy.

None of us are perfect leaders, but we do a ton of conscious leadership training.

FILE UNDER CONTINUOUS LEARNING

What Pitzo has learned over the years is that, as long as all information is accessible to all employees, no matter the language they speak, employees will get behind the same organizational goals. Different backgrounds can come together to solve issues, and, perhaps most importantly, you may run into crises that you weren't expecting to find on a factory floor, such as providing some staff with parenting guidance. It's important not to ignore these crises, but to embrace them. At the end of the crisis, both the employee and company will come out better, together, on the other side.

PART 3: MINDSET

Mindset empowers us to be a catalyst for change. A vision for our team combined with resilient leadership sets the tone for the competitive positioning conversation. Rethinking our approach to the future amidst ongoing change is a good way of ensuring our place on the global stage. Hello, organizational success is now undeniably in your line of sight.

Chapter 8

A LOOK AT WHAT'S NEXT

Stay curious, then keep going.

In today's competitive, ever-changing economic environment, it's hard to know what's around the corner, even in the short-term. However, forecasting future requirements is imperative.

In terms of future workforce needs, IMEC is helping to bridge the manufacturing skills gap through various approaches including a pilot skills gap analysis project. The program is aimed to help participating manufacturers plan their future workforce requirements and strengthen their communities. Why is this important for Illinois manufacturers? One of the biggest issues for managers in the manufacturing sector today is knowing what information and skills workers will need beyond today's work. We've seen the same series of events occur across many of our client companies: changing customer preferences lead to new products, which then leads to changing the way work is done.

The skills gap analysis project involved six Chicago-area manufacturing companies who understand that defining future workforce requirements is critical to sustaining competitiveness. The companies followed a specific process to identify the current and forecasted duties and tasks of a job, with the intent that the resulting information will guide future workforce planning.

The project was headed by Dr. Ronald Jacobs, professor of Human Resource Development, University of Illinois, Urbana-Champaign. He commented, "Much of what we know about job requirements is based on using a set of systematic techniques to analyze the work. Until now, most of the techniques focus on what is occurring now on jobs, not necessarily on what may be occurring in the near future. Many manufacturing companies have a sense of their near-term workforce needs based on what products they might be bidding on or what new technologies they will likely need to invest in. The project is a great opportunity to implement what we already know about analyzing work, but now putting it all together in a new way."

Reshoring is yet another hot topic for Illinois manufacturers. An article by Forbes likens it to the consumer trend of "farm-to-table," stating: "In the future, manufacturers will want to build where they sell for several reasons, including faster time to market, lower working capital, government policies, and increased resiliency."[35]

Many of the ideas explored in *Made in Illinois* directly relate to reimagining the future of manufacturing: leading with vision, improving workplace culture, inspiring long-term customer relationships, leveraging the supply chain, striving for operational excellence, investing in technology, and readying for the unexpected. Forging a path for what lies ahead does not mean having a crystal ball, but rather a crystal clear view of where you need to be on the global stage. In the *IndustryWeek Special Research Report* entitled "The Future of Manufacturing: 2020 and Beyond," we see this confirmed: " . . . any US manufacturer and factory that has survived over the past several decades has to be globally competitive. They have no choice."

Anticipating the future is part science, part art, maybe even a small part luck. One thing we know for sure, though: when manufacturers look outside their factories, share ideas with other manufacturers, talk to customers, and collaborate to find bigger solutions, global competitiveness becomes achievable. In this chapter, we look at the rapid rise of production ahead and why overseas markets need the products and ingenuity of small, midsize, and large Illinois manufacturers.

PREPARING EMPLOYEES FOR RAPID INCREASE IN PRODUCTION

During times of rapid change, it is easy to lose sight of the organization's longer-term needs. Take the time to slow down and assess your organization's strengths and challenges to upscale quickly with employees who are clear about your mission and vision.

Strong leaders will align organizational goals and values with daily activities. Involving employees and getting their input into where the organization is headed holds many great, often unexpected, benefits. People naturally get behind initiatives when they've been asked to provide their personal insights.

Employee engagement at all levels drives productivity. Below are suggestions to guide resource allocation and enhance efficiencies with the side benefit of improving employee engagement and readiness for the future. Many of the tools you've read about in previous chapters will help you implement these ideas. So, grab your favorite color from your stash of sticky notes, bookmark specific how-to tips, or even bend the pages of your favorite ideas.

Host town hall style meetings with C-level leaders (virtual or in small groups). Using empathy, showing appreciation, involving each other in solutions, and asking questions go a long way to enhancing both personal and organizational connections.

Distribute a quick, five-question online survey to employees. Include questions on strategy, process improvements, and wish list items that would help everyone do their jobs more efficiently. What unnecessary frustrations do employees face? What barriers can be removed? Are there improvements that are easier to make than others?

Identify critical positions within your organization and create job breakdowns that will enable cross-training. Identify pockets of tribal knowledge and lead these individuals through a constructive brain dump. Create efficient breakdowns from this intel, including specific tasks, key points, important steps, and safety measures.

Clean and organize. We all work smarter in an orderly space. This enables your team to improve their efficiency and productivity. It also gives everyone the feeling of a fresh perspective. Clean and organize office spaces, pitch dated files, and empty drawers of accumulated junk.

Be on the lookout for hidden talents within your workforce. Adversity is the mother of invention. Be open to suggestions and ask employees how their skills can contribute to organizational goals. Inspire employee engagement and satisfaction.

OPPORTUNITIES ARE HIGH FOR SMALL AND MIDSIZE MANUFACTURERS IN ILLINOIS TO SELL OVERSEAS

In basketball, you have to take the shot if you want to score. The same principle applies to global sales channels and creating top line growth (aka points on the board). So, where do Illinois manufacturers rank in selling outside the US and what are our future opportunities?

According to the Office of the United States Trade Representative, in 2018, Illinois goods exports were $65.5 billion, 22% ($12 billion) higher compared to 2008. Also, in 2018, Illinois was the sixth largest state exporter of goods with goods exported accounting for 7.6% of Illinois GDP.

Machinery led the list of goods exports followed by chemicals, computer and electronic products, transportation equipment, and food and kindred products.[36]

Understanding the need to connect Illinois manufacturers with global growth opportunities, IMEC has worked with partners to deploy an export-focused program called ExporTech. This nationwide program created by the US Commerce NIST Manufacturing Extension Partnership (MEP) provides personalized coaching to a small group of manufacturers with development of a strategic plan for international sales. Over the course of three months, each company receives custom market research to narrow down their target markets while learning export best practices, payment options, market entry and sales channels, and logistics and shipping.

Twenty-seven Illinois companies have successfully graduated from the ExporTech program since 2016. Here, we interviewed a spokesperson for Vogel Tool & Die. Based in Addison, Vogel Tool & Die began making pipe and tube notchers over eighty years ago. From chain link fences to office furniture, wheelchairs, conveyors, car suspensions, and more, Vogel pipe notchers and other tube fabricating tools are used to manufacture thousands of products you encounter every day.

What did you expect when you signed up for ExporTech?

ExporTech was so much more than I expected. I thought I would walk away with a couple tips and sit through a lot of presentations by businesses pitching their services. I was so surprised and pleased to discover what a well-planned program it is. My personal coach, Bernie Bowersock, had decades of experience and wisdom and the others we worked with, such as the researchers who helped us define new markets, all provided expert level guidance and advice.

The service providers who participated add significant value and focused on education on export-specific tasks and issues as opposed to simply promoting their specific products.

The structure–one in-person meeting per month, plus homework–enabled us, as a very small company, to participate without significant business disruption.

The feedback and shared experience of going through the training with other companies–start-ups and established businesses, both–helped enhance the experience and was a great sounding board for ideas as we all learned together.

What were Vogel's challenges related to export? How did ExporTech help you with these challenges?

Although we had international sales, they were not through any focused plan or the result of concerted efforts on our part. As a small company, we were always too busy dealing with the day-to-day to focus on exporting or to even acknowledge that growing export sales requires a strategy and plan.

First, ExporTech forced us to develop an export-specific business plan, to allocate dollars and resources. To pick countries and specific action items on which we will focus.

Secondly, we were very much in the "we don't know what we don't know" phase. We were unaware of some of the regulatory issues that govern export activities, and ways to reduce our risk by protecting transactions via proper process and policies.

Have you seen any impact to your business after participating in ExporTech?

Because we have a very mature, niche product line that is already well known in the US, we were beginning to experience a domestic sales decline. Without a significant growth in international sales, we would likely have had to lay off several workers.

One country that ExporTech's market research identified as a potential market was the UK. Vogel Tool & Die began a marketing campaign targeting the country and interestingly, although we have very few UK inquiries and no new sales yet, we have seen an increase in inquiries from Ireland, Scotland, and New Zealand. We have had one prospective customer from Ireland visit our factory and a prospective dealer fly in from New Zealand.

Any suggestions for companies considering participating in ExporTech?

Do get buy-in from upper management and a commitment to be involved in the ExporTech program, and don't simply send a shipping clerk or sales assistant. Do budget time to participate in the three in-person classes, and to complete the homework. The homework should spur robust discussion on the pros and cons of various strategies and how these exporting strategies fit into your overall business plan. Do share-as-you-go with others in the company not actively participating in the training.

Chapter 9

RESILIENCY AT EVERY LEVEL

Play the long game.

Most of us recognize Newton's first law of motion. In short, it says objects resist change to their state of motion, tending to "keep on keeping on." If at rest, they stay that way. If in motion, they keep going. According to this law, this holds true until a new external force acts upon the object, forcing it to alter its current state.

Sleep-deprived manufacturing leaders know this law all too well. Driving change for the better calls for resiliency, that grit to stay the course even when it's hard.

As we've learned from Newton's Law, without an overwhelming influx of energy, the average human will "keep on doing what we've always done." Effective leaders know they must input tremendous amounts of personal energy, super-human patience, and true emotion into the organization to see challenges through.

In this chapter, we offer up points to consider more than mere advice. How much energy do you invest in doing what you've always done and how much do you invest in change? In what manner does your team handle change? And, how will you build a culture of resilience and inspire leaders who play the long game no matter the onslaught of challenge?

We leave you with more questions than answers, mainly because we are confident the answers are inside you and the direction in which your organization is headed.

On to our discussion about change and the shaping of resiliency . . .

YOU AS A CHANGE LEADER

Leading change well is one of the most important talents you bring to your organization. Change, for the most part, is inevitable: industry evolves, buying habits change, new technology surfaces, markets fluctuate, and crises occur. How you handle change–how you inspire others to adapt and grow through change–helps determine the outcome on the other side of that change.

In some cases, when leaders ask employees to change the way they do things, some employees are offended. Others are surprised by a level of care they've not experienced first-hand from a leader before. Take note of how people generally react to change within your organization. Is it positive, negative, or somewhere in between?

Regardless of the reaction spectrum, workflow process, documented steps, gathering insight, and proper training all fall under change leadership.

Of course, we've all witnessed short bursts of change with "do this or else" and "because I said so," but effective leaders know this type of my-way-or-the-highway tactic rarely brings about lasting change and creates a negative culture. Let's look now at four key elements behind positive change management.

Willingness to change. Leadership creates openness to change through the leader's own determined energy, clear and consistent messaging, a cadre of frontline supporters, and diligence to the cause. The degree to which they care about the employees and the business influences another person's willingness to change.

Because openness to change differs for every employee, it is up to leadership to create consistent messaging, consistently walk the talk, and to listen to employees' concerns and act on them.

Leaders should *clearly and specifically* articulate their own personal willingness to change early on in any change process; in other words, they need to personally share with as many employees as possible why they believe these changes are truly necessary. This calls for you to inspire others and talk about the change both logically and emotionally. Like many leaders, Nestlé CEO, Mark Schneider, wrote a letter to colleagues in 2020, outlining some of the changes underway. In closing, he wrote:

> "Let me add a personal note. Along with everyone else at Nestlé I am working hard to cope with this crisis. We–

> and I–will be with you every step of the way. Like most of you I also have a family to worry about. I am a Nestlé colleague, but also a father, a husband and a son. At times like these, the worry list can be long for all of us, there are no exceptions. But I am also convinced that we will get through this, if we do not lose our self-confidence and our energy. It is literally in our hands."[37]

Mr. Schneider brought the pragmatic side of change to a personal level and shared his own worldview so that those reading his letter knew there was a human heart behind the message.

With transparent, face-to-face communication, leaders help constituents understand WHY the change is truly necessary. The effective leader also puts the "why" along with the "how" into videos, speeches, and written statements that they stand behind in thought, word, and action. When members of your leadership team find one another acting in inconsistent ways, call each other out and talk through these inconsistencies until intentions become reality. Share stories that motivate others on how it can be better when everyone is on board. If key leaders are not infused with the intense energy required to change people's behaviors, and they shy away from potential conflict, the change process remains underpowered.

Skill to change. In addition to consistent messaging, employees also need training in new practices. Change leaders provide the necessary training, never assuming people will know what to do and how to do it.

Great leaders provide not only information to read, messages to listen to, but also demonstrations on the right and wrong way. They provide opportunities for employees to practice new behaviors and receive feedback. They provide accountability reminders so that the ever-present human factor, forgetfulness, has trouble taking hold. For example, there is a right way to wear a face mask and many other risky ways that could result in infection.

Coaching for accountability. Coaching is handled through communication and feedback. This is why a majority of the best companies begin every shift, every meeting, every small gathering, with a safety tip. We are creatures of habit! We need constant reminders to provide the influx of new energy that will drive change forward. Consistent messaging and feedback from executives, supervisors, team leads, mentors, and fellow operators increases energy toward the change. Knowing that your coworkers are watching your behaviors and giving you feedback each week motivates you to make the changes you've all committed to.

If necessary, use outside professionals to coach and act as accountability partners. Many IMEC clients confess that simply because they knew we would be on site to check in, they felt accountable to dig back into the new tools and sharpen their application.

Finally, the reward. With all this energy going into the work of change, we may forget about reward. Leaders who want sustained change reward employees along the way. They reward themselves and their team. With an eye on the change, keep rewards simple but consistent. You've heard the phrase "catch 'em doing something right"? A simple "thank you," "way to go," or "you're doing great," can go a long way toward making a tired team feel good. Reward is very personal, so ask employees what celebration would look like for them. Ask early and ask often.

In short, at the outset of any change–even something as small and straight forward as how to wear a face mask–you as a leader have an enormous *push up the hill* with personal energy that may cause a few sleepless nights. Check the change plan for the four elements–will, skill, coaching, and reward–to make sure all essentials are included. As any leader who has undergone the intense internal and emotional pressure required to reach the other side can attest, it will be well worth the effort. Former GE CEO, the late Jack Welch, summed it up this way: "Change before you have to." Indeed.

SEVEN ESSENTIAL TRAITS FOR BUILDING RESILIENCY

Disruption and economic downturn can happen to any company, at any time. Disruptions can be intimidating, but companies that invest thought and resources into contingency planning and continuous improvement are often better positioned to respond to adversity. They are resilient, and your manufacturing company can be, too.

So, let's look at what makes resilient companies different:

1. **Astute situational awareness.** Many companies are oblivious to changes around them while an

equal number become frozen because they don't know how to adapt. Leaders–be aware, alert, and engaged. This means talking to suppliers in the market segments you serve. Constant awareness of what is coming helps companies avoid being blindsided. The OODA loop–observe, orient, decide, and act–is a useful tool. Taking these words a little deeper, you observe the current situation, orient yourself to where you want to go, decide on a path and how to handle challenges, and act on the plan to implement your decisions. Planning a growth strategy and driving change takes time and structure. Market analysis, structured product development, and consistent marketing and sales efforts make all the difference.

2. **Leverage organizational competencies.** Why do companies buy from you instead of other suppliers? Your strengths are important, but they shouldn't be all you think about. Resting on your strengths can be profitable but may lead to stagnation. Companies that need to reboot and recapture the spirit of innovation can find a SWOT analysis (strengths, weaknesses, opportunities, and threats) helpful. It's a great tool for sparking a critical dialogue with diverse members of your team (healthy debate leads to innovation). It's also important to talk to customers and suppliers to get external perspective (plus, it's a nice break from day-to-day demands). Talking to these folks can instantly clarify opportunities such

as problems your firm can solve. A single success such as meeting a customer's need can transform your company culture and your employees into innovative problem-solvers.

3. **A growth strategy should be as unique as the business it serves.** When you experience a downturn, how do you keep the business going and people employed? The Doblin Model is a tool that helps companies think through the core elements of how they add value. Think ideation and innovation. By using a set of more than 100 cards (color-coded and easy to use: fun!), you can enrich existing and new products. The Doblin Model helps create insights about your competition and makes it easy to spot missing dimensions that will strengthen your product. Recognizing core elements and envisioning complementary products and services helps diversify and pursue an incredibly rapid path to innovation.
4. **Measure and manage thoughtful action.** Keep your company on track and moving forward with key performance indicators (remember SMART goals in chapter five?). We've seen many smaller manufacturers struggle to put structure around how they target new opportunities and audiences. SMART goals provide a structured pathway to lead generation and diversification. Market scouting (more on this in a bit) relies on structure, goals, and transparency with your team.

5. **Connecting individuals with opportunities.** Make connections that lead to growth. Imagine new markets and new audience and go a step further to identify the individuals that you hold in high regard in those markets. You know your company can add value, so communicate that to the right people in the right markets. Build their trust, and you'll be positioned for success when you're ready to expand. And, don't forget current customers. Review your list of customers and their market segments and then prioritize the path toward increased sales with a spirit of resilience.
6. **Adapt quickly to changing conditions.** This is a cousin to situational awareness. Markets change quickly. Customers find other suppliers. It happens. Market scouting is a process that helps you face adversity with structure. You test a hypothesis to see if it's the best way forward. Market scouting involves getting your ideas in front of the people you think will benefit from them, and then tracking data from these interviews to identify opportunities. In other words, you come up with an idea and take it directly to potential end users to see if they would use it (no stopping you now). Market scouting is a rapid-fire way to move forward if you think your existing core competencies match the needs of other industries.
7. **A resilient growth strategy energizes the culture of a workplace.** Companies that succeed have a culture rooted in resilience. If people in your

organization love what they do, they will do their best. If they see your company is innovative, they'll be innovative. The path of continuous improvement is contagious, and it makes your company a very desirable place to work. Attracting the best talent means sustaining growth. You really can't overstate the impact an energized workplace has on manufacturing. The role of being resilient doesn't fall on one person–it's not just the CEO's responsibility. Your company's culture should be one of resilience and problem-solving. With that, tremendous growth follows.

Where Should You Start?

Take the first step forward that feels most comfortable for your organization. For many companies, that might be a customer survey, contacting past customers to see how you can earn their business back, or following up with prospects who never converted into customers. Create opportunities by asking customers what is next for them and how you can help.

Complacency poses the biggest risk of all. Create a resilient growth strategy. Work with your team–from leadership to those on the shop floor–and your customers. Build resiliency and innovation into your company's culture so if market or customer demand suddenly changes, you can adapt and thrive regardless of the circumstances.

IMEC wishes to thank Katie Rapp, Writer/Editor for NIST's Manufacturing Extension Partnership, for contributing to Made in Illinois.

DEVELOPING RESILIENT LEADERS

No matter what is happening in the background, look steadfastly toward your company's future. You may not have a clear vision of what lies ahead; however, you will be more proactive in shaping the story you step into.

Developing resilient leaders profoundly impacts future organizational success.

Here's why. First, you will have a stronger bench ready to help you weather disruption. Second, you will reduce stress and provide motivation for employees. If a company is willing to allocate resources toward development, people know they have a future with the organization.

Here are steps to consider:

Identify leaders and emerging leaders in your business. By including your emerging leaders, you are bulking up your talent and creating a relief valve for current leaders.

Assess the skill sets of every individual within the identified leadership group. Match skill sets against the skills you identified that will allow your company to be successful moving forward. It is quite likely that needed skills have shifted over the past couple of months and there are some new gaps (change is the one thing that never changes!). Connect with employees and address their personal needs as well as their practical needs.

Identify resources that provide interactive online training. Online training and meeting platforms are very sophisticated. A good trainer will be able to provide learning, engagement, and skill practice using digital platforms.

Reinforce the learned skill. Just like classroom learning, following up is the best way to ensure adoption. Work with each learner to establish their individual development goals, then follow up after the training to assess and encourage them to put their new skills to use.

Develop your leaders now, so they will be ready to chart a course for tomorrow. Just as we began our conversation, we close with a mention of organizational success. Each little nugget shared in *Made in Illinois* is meant to help you advance with measurable progress, small and big wins alike, and excellence as only you define it. In the foreword to *Modern Manufacturing Volume 2*, Kerry Baskins writes: "The great differentiator in business is when an organization steps out and creates value from something never tried before."[38]

Resilient leaders are willing to fail and learn and try again. They see opportunity where others see problems. For many Illinois manufacturers, this kind of grit has long defined generations of makers and will continue to fuel the future of industry in Illinois.

CLOSING THOUGHTS: THE LESSONS WE LEARN MAKE US FIERCER COMPETITORS

by Dr. David Boulay, President of IMEC

THE FUTURE DEPENDS ON WHAT YOU DO TODAY.
– *Mahatma Gandhi*

We have experienced enough in our careers to understand that change is an unpredictable guarantee. One way or another we adapt to this constant barrage of customer change orders, competitor shifts, key employee departures, new technology, regulatory changes, and much more. We navigate the occasional major shifts from gaining or losing the biggest customer to dealing with a plant emergency or natural disaster. We weather the storms of massive societal challenges like the Great Recession or the pandemic, which shake not only our business, but our industries, to the core.

The frequency and pace of change appears to increase exponentially. It can feel like we suffer through random acts of uncontrolled chaos at times. In all cases, we take responsibility to apply our experiences and maneuver through these external influences. We must be the calm in all the storms.

We address these challenges best through the proactive steps to improve and refine best practices each day. We do our preventative maintenance for our car by regularly changing the oil, checking the tires, filters, battery, and washer fluid. We do regular home maintenance and improvements to continually adjust and accommodate to our needs. Similarly, our business is best prepared through constant tinkering and adjustment before the problem occurs. That's how we lead.

Five core building blocks ensure a team's commitment and attitude to accelerate competitiveness. These attributes are: being results driven, collaboration, agility, learning, and passion. We believe in these traits so much at IMEC that they are our core values. They blend to produce meaningful and lasting success.

It starts with passion. The pride of leaders is deeply rooted. It is on display during any plant tour or when you ask a business leader "How's business?" In return, you will hear energizing stories and insights about the history, the important roles that each manufactured part serves, the talent, the machines, the process flow, and the community engagement. We all feel the energy from the pride and enthusiasm in delivering on a core purpose.

It is unsurprising this passion nurtures the natural desire to focus on transforming raw materials into finished goods. We are pleased when the final product is ready to ship. We are delighted when a satisfied customer says, *"Job well done."* We are ecstatic when we see our products in everyday use making society better. It all reinforces our passion. Harnessing this passion creates the endurance to succeed even in the most trying times.

This passion gets needed direction by being results-driven. Performance dashboards and financial statements keep us working on things that matter. At times, others may think we are hard-nosed, tight with our spending, uncompromising, and carry high expectations for achievement. Rather, it is just our passion focused on results. At the heart of these perceptions is our drive to deliver meaningful outcomes in all endeavors. This does mean watching the bottom line, being detailed oriented, and holding others accountable. Rarely connected to being results-driven, but perhaps most vital, is also being agile. Results are a compromise of many options, and it requires the agility to choose.

Just ask cats. Cats can teach us a lot about agility. We have two cats–Kimchi and Nabbi–that are incredibly passionate about their laser pointer. They patiently wait for me to sit in the assigned spot. And, with a click of the switch, the laser dot chase ensues. I move the laser in unpredictable paths. Slow. Fast. Shaky. Steady. On the floor. On the wall. The cats prepare. They crouch down. Ears tucked. They focus. Focus. Focus. Pounce. As the dot scurries away, their acrobatic talents shine. They catch the dot over and over no matter the direction or speed. They retain an incredible will to succeed, an eye on the prize, and the agility to perform.

Business agility is essential to achieve results. Much like our feline friends, our acrobatic talents facilitate being responsive and flexible to stakeholder needs and changing conditions. But it is less about the hero employee jumping through hoops at the last minute to get an order out the door. Rather, it is our processes, standard and consistent work ethic, and deep knowledge and talent that make us agile. Because agility happens through our core stability. From this core we can adapt, create, and shift. Agility creates strength and allows us to be resilient.

Business agility also happens through collaboration. Take a few minutes for a thought experiment. Imagine running your whole business by yourself. Imagine doing each task in sequence from beginning to end. Sell the order, enter information into the system, run every machine, deliver to the customer, and everything in between. Include personally doing every task your suppliers undertake to give you the required inputs. It is likely you can figure it all out over time. Yet, it would not take long to realize the effort would be slow, ineffective, and error prone. There would be little agility to deal with any change.

Phrases like 'teamwork makes the dream work' and 'there's no I in team' may feel a bit corny at times, but they are truisms to create results and adapt to changing needs. The ways in which we collaborate are how we produce impactful results and adapt to change. Our workforce, suppliers, customers, vendors, and others are all contributors to our successful endeavor. Collaboration facilitates agility and the focus on results.

Finally, learning supercharges collaboration and agility and powers up our passion. Acquiring and sharing knowledge that helps us succeed means gaining insights and attempting new ideas to improve. We create greater value over time through learning. Our expertise grows. Our perceived value rises. Learning naturally sparks questions, conversations, and debates. We deepen collaboration and find ways to perform our work in new ways creating greater agility and better results.

We hope *Made in Illinois* feeds your learning by

presenting best practices in actionable, bite-sized pieces. Leaders facing a hectic and urgent pace of work can embrace quick learning moments. Taking the aha moments gained and trying them in the business will proactively prepare us for the inevitable change and challenges we will face.

Makers have always led the way. This will not change. Harnessing our passion, driving results through agility, collaboration, and learning will guide you well. The leader mindset brings together the people to focus on performance.

1. You create the direction to best serve customers and other stakeholders.
2. The team applies their knowledge, skills, talent, and technology to achieve the goals.
3. Everyone focuses on developing and always improving efficient and effective processes and products.

This is the way to accelerate your competitiveness in a forever changing landscape. We owe it to ourselves, our employees and their families, and our communities to frequently pause, reflect, adapt, and reposition for success.

This is what makers have always done. This is what will carry us forward.

NOTES

PREFACE: PLAYING THE LONG GAME BY DR. DAVID BOULAY, PRESIDENT OF IMEC

1. Founders Online, a website co-created by the National Archives and the University of Virginia Press, https://founders.archives.gov/documents/Hamilton/01-10-02-0001-0007

1. LEADERS, HOW DO YOU DEFINE EXCELLENCE?

2. Matteo Mancini, Wiktor Namysł, Rafael Pardo, and Sree Ramaswamym, "Global Growth, Local Roots: The Shift Toward Emerging Markets," McKinsey & Company, August 30, 2017, https://www.mckinsey.com/business-functions/operations/our-insights/global-growth-local-roots-the-shift-toward-emerging-markets
3. Matteo Mancini, Wiktor Namysł, Rafael Pardo, and Sree Ramaswamym.
4. oshua Ball, "Emerging Economies Will Hold Increasing Amounts Of Global Economic Power By 2050," *Global Security Review*, June 10, 2019, https://globalsecurityreview.com/will-global-economic-order-2050-look-like/
5. Ian Colotia, Will Kletter, Michael McAdoo, and Justin Rose, "A Manufacturing Strategy Built for Trade Instability," Boston Consulting Group, February 13, 2020, https://www.bcg.com/publications/2020/manufacturing-strategy-built-trade-instability

6. Union of Japanese Scientists and Engineers, "History of the Deming Prize," http://www.juse.or.jp/deming_en/award/01.html
7. Baldrige Foundation website, https://baldrigefoundation.org/what-we-do/our-impact/economic-impact.html#:~:text=The%20Bureaus%20of%20Economic%20Analysis,than%20matched%20industries%3B%20and%20growth
8. Mike Hoban, "Navigating COVID-19: Using Key Principals in a Crisis," DDI, April 2, 2020, https://www.ddiworld.com/blog/key-principles-in-a-crisis
9. Development Dimensions International, 2019.
10. "Employee Empowerment in the Workplace: Definition & Best Practices," Smarp, December 19, 2019, https://blog.smarp.com/empowerment-in-the-workplace-enable-your-employees
11. Naz Beheshti, "10 Timely Statistics About the Connection Between Employment Engagement and Wellness," *Forbes*, 2018.
12. Naz Beheshti.
13. "Corporate Efforts to Bolster Diversity and Inclusion in the Workplace are Intensifying," PwC, https://www.pwc.com/us/en/industries/industrial-products/library/diversity-inclusion-in-manufacturing.html
14. Kellie Wong, "Diversity and Inclusion in the Workplace," Achievers blog, September 14, 2020, https://www.achievers.com/blog/diversity-and-inclusion/#:~:text=Kellie%20Wong&text=Gartner%20found%20that%20inclusive%20teams,to%20their%20less%20diverse%20counterparts

15. Lydia Dishman, "The Business Case for Women in the C-Suite," Fast Company, July 9, 2015, https://www.fastcompany.com/3048342/the-business-case-for-women-in-the-c-suite
16. US Bureau of Labor Statistics, https://www.bls.gov/cps/cpsaat18.html

2. WORKFORCE AND CULTURE: COMPETING GLOBALLY STARTS AT HOME

17. Wikipedia, https://en.wikipedia.org/wiki/Training_Within_Industry
18. Randall J. Beck and Jim Harter, "Why Great Managers are so Rare," Gallup, https://www.gallup.com/workplace/231593/why-great-managers-rare.aspx#:~:text=Managers%20account%20for%20at%20least,severely%20low%20worldwide%20employee%20engagement
19. Neil Burton, "Our Hierarchy of Needs," *Psychology Today,* May 23, 2012, https://www.psychologytoday.com/us/blog/hide-and-seek/201205/our-hierarchy-needs
20. R. Scott Russell, "Improving Safety Through Employee Engagement," C.A. Short, https://www.cashort.com/blog/employee-engagement-is-key-to-improving-workplace-safety-0#:~:text=It%20concluded%20that%20engaged%20employees,their%20commitment%20to%20employee%20engagement
21. N.F. Mendoza, "Best Practices: The Top 13 Ways to

Manage Remote Workers," *TechRepublic,* December 9, 2019, https://www.techrepublic.com/index.php/article/best-practices-the-top-13-ways-to-manage-remote-employees/

22. Carmine Gallo, "Neuroscience Proves You Should Follow TED's 18-Minute Rule to Win Your Pitch," *Inc.,* February 21, 2017, https://www.inc.com/carmine-gallo/why-your-next-pitch-should-follow-teds-18-minute-rule.html
23. "Fast Facts and Trends for B2B and High Consideration Purchase Marketers," LoSasso, https://www.losasso.com/wp-content/uploads/2019/06/Fast-facts-and-trends-for-B2B-and-high-consideration-purchase-marketers.pdf

3. THE VALUE OF CUSTOMER RELATIONSHIPS

24. American Marketing Association website, https://www.ama.org/the-definition-of-marketing-what-is-marketing/#:~:text=Definition%20of%20Brand,from%20those%20of%20other%20sellers
25. Chigbo Ezumba, "Voice of the Customer: A Tool for Continual Improvement," *Quality Magazine,* March 1, 2017, https://www.qualitymag.com/articles/93851-voice-of-the-customer-a-tool-for-continual-improvement#:~:text=According%20to%20the%20ASQ%20Quality,process%20for%20capturing%20cu-stomers'%20requirements

4. THE MODERN SUPPLY CHAIN AS A COMPETITIVE EDGE

26. MIT Center for Transportation and Logistics website, https://ctl.mit.edu/about/bio/jonathan-byrnes
27. Daniel Stanton's LinkedIn post, "Best Supply Chain Quotes," LinkedIn, June 8, 2019, https://www.linkedin.com/pulse/best-supply-chain-quotes-daniel-stanton/
28. Willy C. Shih, "Global Supply Chains in a Post-Pandemic World," *Harvard Business Review,* September-October 2020, https://hbr.org/2020/09/global-supply-chains-in-a-post-pandemic-world

5. ACHIEVING OPERATIONAL EXCELLENCE

29. Susan McQuillan M.S., RDN, "Why Do Humans Resist Change?" *Psychology Today*, October 21, 2020, https://www.psychologytoday.com/us/blog/cravings/201910/why-do-humans-resist-change
30. Nadeem Huaddi, "Why Do We Call It a 'Dashboard'?," TheHogRing.com, November 25, 2012, https://www.thehogring.com/2012/11/25/where-did-the-term-dashboard-come-from/#:~:text=The%20word%20%E2%80%9Cdashboard%E2%80%9D%20was%20originally,mud%20flaps%20for%20horses'%20hooves

6. INTEGRATING TECHNOLOGY FOR GREATER PROCESS INNOVATION

31. Karen Harris, Austin Kimson and Andrew Schwedel, "Labor 2030: The Collision of Demographics, Automation and Inequality," Bain & Company, February 7, 2018, https://www.bain.com/insights/labor-2030-the-collision-of-demographics-automation-and-inequality/#:~:text=The%20rapid%20spread%20of%20automation,growth%20for%20many%20more%20workers
32. "Industrial Internet of Things, Wikipedia, https://en.wikipedia.org/wiki/Industrial_internet_of_things
33. Randi Golan, "Why SMBs are Under-Prepared for Cyberattacks," Mimecast blog, July 21, 2020, https://www.mimecast.com/blog/why-smbs-are-under-prepared-for-cyberattacks/

7. COMPETING DURING CRISIS: RESPOND, RECOVER, REBOUND

34. William Arthur Ward was an American motivational writer, Wikipedia, "William Arthur Ward," https://en.wikipedia.org/wiki/William_Arthur_Ward

8. A LOOK AT WHAT'S NEXT

35. Amar Hanspel, "Five Predictions For the manufacturing Industry in 2021," *Forbes,* December 7, 2020, https://

www.forbes.com/sites/amarhanspal/2020/12/07/five-predictions-for-the-manufacturing-industry-in-2021/?sh=35ffdc9528ca

36. Office of the United States Trade Representative, https://ustr.gov/map/state-benefits/il#:~:text=Made%2Din%2DAmerica%20Manufacturing%20Exports%20from%20Illinois%20and%20Jobs&text=Other%20top%20manufacturing%20exports%20are,kindred%-20products%20(%244.1%20billion)

9. RESILIENCY AT EVERY LEVEL

37. Mark Schneider, "A Message from our CEO to Employees," Nestlé website, March 23, 2020, https://www.nestle.com/media/news/covid-19-ceo-message-to-employees

CLOSING THOUGHTS: THE LESSONS WE LEARN MAKE US FIERCER COMPETITORS BY DR. DAVID BOULAY, PRESIDENT OF IMEC

38. Michelle Segrest, "Modern Manufacturing (Volume 2): Real World Stories From the Plant Floor," Navigate Content Inc., 2019, p. 7.

ACKNOWLEDGMENTS

Throughout IMEC's twenty-five years, there are countless stories, successes, and achievements in which we take great pride. These accomplishments are created and celebrated from the 15,280+ projects with thousands of companies with which we have closely interacted. The triumphs that we have experienced are, in no uncertain terms, enhanced by the enduring partnerships, friendships, and organizations with similar missions as IMEC and its commitments to excellence. Good enough has just never been good enough.

Our IMEC team of talented, hard-working, and knowledgeable professionals has faced challenge after challenge in our fast-paced, ever-changing world of manufacturing. Their ability to adjust and seek better, more efficient ways to enhance the growth and capabilities of manufacturers in Illinois is noteworthy and impressive. They demonstrate daily their knowledge, passion, and steadfast commitment to promoting our noble pursuit of economic and workforce competitiveness.

I would be remiss if I did not rejoice in the vital role our IMEC Board has played in the ongoing success of our organization. We have been so very fortunate to have the Board made up of dynamic thought leaders who guide us to set high standards yet ground us in the realities of day-to-day manufacturing. The Board has consistently inspired and motivated us by being champions of the IMEC vision and mission. And, they have done so in thoughtful and encouraging ways that ignite us to be our best selves.

Our university partners (Bradley University, Northern Illinois University, Southern Illinois University and University of Illinois at Chicago) have also been our steady and steadying foundations over the years. These four schools have provided us with unwavering support and have enabled IMEC to be and become bigger than we could have been otherwise.

The US Department of Commerce NIST Manufacturing Extension Partnership (MEP) is the reason for IMEC's existence. This federal program, with its mission to support the transfer of manufacturing technology to improve productivity and technological capabilities of America's manufacturers, has always pointed us in the direction of bolstering the success of companies and the upskilling of their workforce.

Our friends and partners have been essential collaborators who have committed to similar goals. The manufacturing associations, the workforce boards, the local economic development agencies, the community colleges, and the state's key government leaders have been with us with sleeves rolled up and boots on the ground where the actual work happens. These partners provide living proof that the whole is greater than the sum of its parts.

The true inspiration for IMEC is the manufacturing leaders and their workforce. They are the reason for our passion. They are the reason we strive for excellence. They are the reason we work so hard to create the environment for them to be the makers.

This book got over the finish line because of the coaching, motivating, support, and confidence provided by the K+L Storytellers team, Michele and Roderick Kelly.

A special thanks goes to them for guiding us through to completion. We just thought we had a bunch of really good thought pieces and blog posts, but Michele and Roderick convinced us that we, in fact, had the responsibility to tell an important story.

ABOUT IMEC

The Illinois Manufacturing Excellence Center is a team of improvement specialists and technicians dedicated to providing organizations in Illinois with the tools and techniques to create sustainable competitive futures. We work closely with clients to plan critical business improvements in the areas of leadership, strategy, customer engagement, operations, workforce, and measurement of results.

With more than fifty full-time staff and partners statewide, IMEC delivers local expertise to compete globally from planning to implementation and evaluation of client improvements.

IMEC is a proud member of the Manufacturing Extension Partnership (MEP) National Network with access to local and national resources designed to strengthen an organization's competitiveness and position them on a path to excellence. Our goal is to make a significant impact for Illinois manufacturers and innovators. For context, in 2020 alone, we assisted approximately 1,144 Illinois companies, and helped create and retain 6,176 jobs while contributing an aggregate impact to the state's economy of $646,455,900. As a result, IMEC has demonstrated a return on investment that exceeds 19:1. This is made possible as organizations excel toward enterprise excellence.

On a larger scale, the MEP Network has made immense contributions to US manufacturing. Since its inception in 1988, the network has helped 102,443 manufacturers, generated $127.3 billion in sales, and created 1,107,346 jobs across the country.

THE IMEC TEAM

- Jeff Allspaugh*
- Lori Amerman
- Shankar Anant*
- John Azara
- Margo Barr
- Melissa Basa
- Ashley Beaudoin*
- Holly Bender*
- David Boulay*
- John Bradarich
- Jesse Brady*
- Amy Clary*
- Gretchen Clifton
- Stacey Curry
- Glenn Edwards
- Simone Erskine*
- Greg Ferketich*
- Jim Floyd*
- Michelle Fossett
- Mikel Garrett
- Vickie Griffin
- Mary Hallock*
- Jim Hancock
- Dean Harms*
- Amanda Hawley
- Ed Huey
- Kristy Johns*
- Lisa Kenney*
- Shayla Kripalani
- Ben Krupowicz*
- Ryan Langdon*
- Eddie Leach
- Emily Lee
- Mark Loscudo
- Mike Lyle*
- Dave Madden*
- Denisse Manzanilla
- Tim Maurer
- Mary Mechler*
- Mike Monahan
- Maria Moran*
- Dave Musgrave
- Rob Newbold
- Doug Pennington
- Patrick Peplowski
- John Remsey*
- Joanne Romero
- Steve Sandercock
- Stephen Schiera
- Jordyn Shawhan*
- Shannon Shrum
- Jeremy Smith
- Linda Su
- Greg Thompson*
- Hanoz Umrigar*
- Mike Waight*
- Rick Winkler*
- Ken Wunderlich*
- Melissa Zirbel

*Asterisk denotes contributing authors to *Made in Illinois*

MADE IN ILLINOIS READING LIST

The books below were mentioned in *Made in Illinois.* Enjoy!

- *Lincoln on Leadership* by Donald T. Phillips, p. 24
- *Mapping Experiences: A Complete Guide to Creating Value through Journeys, Blueprints, and Diagrams* by Jim Kalbach, p. 88
- *The 80/20 Principle* by Richard Koch, p. 98
- *Guerrilla Marketing* by Jay Conrad Levinson, p. 100
- *The 7 Habits of Highly Effective People* by Stephen Covey, p. 134
- *The Adventures of Sherlock Holmes* by Arthur Conan Doyle, p. 142
- *Modern Manufacturing, Volume 2* by Kerry Baskins, p. 237

PUTTING YOUR PLAYBOOK INTO ACTION

On behalf of everyone at IMEC, we thank you for reading *Made in Illinois.* If there is one thing we wish to leave you with, it's this: you're not alone in your journey.

You, the Illinois manufacturer, have everyone on the IMEC team behind you. Plus, as part of the US Department of Commerce National Institute of Standards and Technology's Manufacturing Extension Partnership (NIST MEP), you have a MEP in every state and in Puerto Rico you can tap into. Consider us part of your pit crew (because every world-class competitor has experts in the wings!). This network gives you access to well over 100,000 staff members and even more partners and third-party experts to help you solve problems, whether those problems are related to integrating technology into your factory floor, filling your hiring gaps, upping your marketing game, or more.

Our mission is to ignite Illinois manufacturing excellence and global competitiveness. We are here to help you solve your toughest manufacturing problems, inspire you to lead with confidence, and support your journey to excellence on a global scale.

Change the game. Compete to win in all you do. We will cheer you to the finish line and beyond.

To inquire about collaborative opportunities, programs or having an IMEC expert speak at your next event, please contact us 888-806-4632 or info@imec.org or visit us at www.imec.org any time.

You can also learn more about NIST's MEP network at https://www.nist.gov/mep, or learn more about the Baldrige criteria at https://baldrige-foundation.org/.